WHAT IS GESTALT THERAPY?

WHAT IS GESTALT THERAPY?

Edited by

Joen Fagan and Irma Lee Shephard

PERENNIAL LIBRARY
Harper & Row, Publishers
New York, Evanston, San Francisco, London

To Fritz . . . a profound and disturbing teacher

Chapters 1–6 comprised Part I and Chapter 7 appeared in Part III of *Gestalt Therapy Now: Theory, Techniques, Applications* which was originally published by Science and Behavior Books, Inc.

WHAT IS GESTALT THERAPY?
Copyright © 1970 by Science and Behavior Books, Inc. All rights reserved. Printed in the United States of America. No part of this book may be used or reproduced in any manner without written permission except in the case of brief quotations embodied in critical articles and reviews. For information address Harper & Row, Publishers, Inc., 10 East 53d Street, New York, N.Y. 10022. Published simultaneously in Canada by Fitzhenry & Whiteside Limited, Toronto.

First PERENNIAL LIBRARY edition published 1973.

STANDARD BOOK NUMBER: 06-080283-9

Designed by Ann Scrimgeour

CONTENTS

Introduction: Theory of Gestalt Therapy ... vii

1. Gestalt Therapy and Gestalt Psychology ... 1
   Richard Wallen

2. Four Lectures ... 11
   Frederick S. Perls

3. Gestalt Therapy: A Behavioristic Phenomenology ... 50
   Elaine Kepner and Lois Brien

4. Present-Centeredness: Technique, Prescription, and Ideal ... 63
   Claudio Naranjo

5. Sensory Functioning in Psychotherapy ... 98
   Erving Polster

6. The Paradoxical Theory of Change ... 110
   Arnold Beisser

7. Crisis Psychotherapy: Person, Dialogue, and the Organismic Event ... 117
   Vincent F. O'Connell

Contributors ... 140

Introduction

THEORY OF GESTALT THERAPY

Introduction
THEORY OF GESTALT THERAPY

Explicit and implicit in the work of any psychotherapist with patients is an underlying theory of personality. The therapist brings to the treatment situation ideas about personality—especially what constitutes good, healthy, satisfying, and valued behavior, and what is inadequate, maladaptive, problem-causing, or self-defeating—as well as ideas about what kinds of experiences and behaviors produce or continue to keep the negatively valued aspects ascendant. The therapist will then utilize procedures or techniques derived from his theory of therapy in order to effect change and to move the person toward more adequate functioning.

Historically, theories of personality have focused on the negative aspects of personality. In part this has been due to the use of the "medical model," which labeled problems in living as "sick" or "pathological" —like illnesses. But medicine has never been interested in health, which is considered only the absence of illness. One of the many costs of using the medical analogy is that we focus mainly on that which we would rather not see. (For example, the early textbooks of personality adjustment devoted most of their emphasis to defense mechanisms and emotional disorders.)

With the development of the "third force" in psychology, which concerns itself with man in his humanness rather than as defined in psychoanalytic or behavioristic terms, and with the beginning of models that view problems in living as difficulties in relating and communicating, there has been a marked shift in interest toward positive aspects of personality and living. Freud's famous statement, "Much has been accomplished if we can change neurotic misery into common unhappiness," is no longer sufficient for most therapists or for the persons requesting their help. Now we use words such as enhancement, intimacy, actualization, creativity, ecstasy, and transcendence to describe what we wish for ourselves and others. The theories of Maslow, Rogers, Jourard, Berne, and others offer as the alternative to misery, not unhappiness, but joy.

Gestalt therapy is strongly allied with this developing position, emphasizing positive directions and goals of living, and using techniques directly and immediately designed to produce them. The implicit message of Gestalt theory as translated into treatment is that there are values in living that persons know from their own experiences or from their observations of others to be valuable and enhancing: spontaneity, sensory awareness, freedom of movement, emotional responsiveness, and expressiveness, enjoyment, ease, flexibility in relating, direct contact and emotional closeness with others, intimacy, competency, immediacy and presence, self-support, and creativity. The patient who comes for help, seeking to relate more

Introduction

adequately with other people and to be able to express his feelings more directly is instructed to express what he is feeling at that moment to another person. The ways in which he stops, blocks, and frustrates himself quickly become apparent, and he can then be assisted in exploring and experiencing the blockings and encouraged to attempt other ways of expressing himself and of relating.

Thus the general approach of Gestalt theory and therapy requires the patient to specify the changes in himself that he desires, assists him in increasing his awareness of how he defeats himself, and aids him in experimenting and changing. Blocks in awareness and behavior emerge in the same way that they manifest themselves in the person's life; his increased awareness of his avoidances and his relief as he becomes able to expand his experience and behavior are felt immediately in increases in capacity for living.

Even though a major contribution of Gestalt therapy has been the close relationship between theory and treatment, this book will initially effect a degree of separation, describing the historical ancestry of Gestalt therapy and presenting theoretical developments in order to provide a basis or "ground" from which techniques and applications can emerge.

The basic principles of Gestalt therapy are largely the work of one man, Frederick S. Perls. After his medical training, Perls was attracted to psychoanalysis; he underwent training analysis and received analytic supervision from several of the well-known "pioneers," including Wilhelm Reich. His education and early professional experiences brought him in contact with Kurt Goldstein and with the ideas of Gestalt psychology and existentialism. He was further influenced by exposure to the brutalizing conditions of World War I, the rejection by other psychoanalysts of his early efforts at contributing to psychoanalytic theory because he challenged the accepted tenets of libido theory, his emigration from Nazi Germany to South Africa, his need there as an army psychiatrist to develop more efficient modes of treatment, and the influences and contributions of his wife, Laura.

"Gestalt Therapy and Gestalt Psychology" (Wallen) identifies some of the ideas and concepts of Gestalt psychology that were adopted by Perls and serve as a cornerstone in his thinking. Gestalt psychology originated as a theory of perception that included the interrelationships between the form of the object and the processes of the perceiver. It was, in part, a reaction to earlier atomistic approaches that attempted to study perception and mental processes by reducing them to elements or mental contents. In contrast, Gestalt thinking emphasized "leaps" of insight, closure, figure-and-ground characteristics, fluidity of perceptual processes, and the perceiver an an active participant in his perceptions rather than a passive recipient of the qualities of form. Wallen describes the normal process of Gestalt formation and destruction, and the processes that interfere with closure or change. He indicates the contributions that Gestalt therapy has made to the theories of Gestalt psychology by extending its concepts to include self-perception, motivation, and the motoric aspects of behavior. Finally, Wallen demonstrates the relevance of Gestalt theory to the operations of the Gestalt therapist.

"Four Lectures" (Perls), which follow, constitute the most extensive statement of Perls's thinking about a number of issues since his basic writings in *Ego,*

INTRODUCTION

Hunger and Aggression and *Gestalt Therapy*. His first lecture begins by noting the split in psychology between the phenomenological approach, with its emphasis on sensation, perception, thinking, and awareness, that is, private behavior, and the behavioristic approach that focuses on observable or public behavior. He then describes four philosophical approaches to the study of behavior: the scientific, which talks *about* behavior with a lack of involvement; the religious and philosophical positions, which emphasize how behavior *should be*—with dissatisfactions; the existential, which focuses on what *is*, but still needs a causal framework; and the Gestalt, which attempts to discover the *how* and *now* of behavior. Freud's contributions to Gestalt therapy include his idea of the unconscious, which Perls translates as describing those aspects of behavior that are unavailable or potential rather than actual, and the concept of thinking as trial work or rehearsing, leading to the Gestalt therapy formulation of anxiety as stage fright.

In contrast to psychoanalysis, Gestalt therapy emphasizes the here and now, with the awareness of experience and varying behaviors. Many people, especially neurotics, avoid experiencing in awareness their self-critical "computing," projecting, or adapting of a variety of other procedures to maintain their usual behaviors. The usual, or status quo, involves holding onto past behavior and roles, or attempting to obtain environmental support by manipulation rather than utilizing self-support. Only by directly experiencing boredom or fear in the present will we find what we attempt to avoid and begin to utilize more of our potentiality.

Perls's second lecture is largely concerned with the

five layers of neurosis. Many people spend much of their time on the first, or *phony*, layer, where we play games, live roles, try to be what we are not, and in the process create voids and disown much of ourselves. We constantly harass ourselves with what Perls calls the "top-dog/under-dog" game where part of ourselves attempts to lecture, urge, and threaten the other part into "good" behavior. The second neurotic layer he calls the *phobic* layer. As we become aware of phony behaviors and manipulations, we begin to get in touch with the fears that maintain them; we experience the wish to avoid new behavior or have fantasies about what the consequences might be if we behaved in a genuine way. The third layer is the *impasse*, where we are caught, not knowing what to do or where to move. We experience the loss of environmental support but do not have the support of belief in our own resources. The fourth stage is the *implosive*, where we may with grief, despair, or self-loathing come to a fuller realization of how we have limited and constricted ourselves; or with fear and doubt we may begin to experiment with new behavior. Following this, the fifth layer, or *explosive*, emerges as the previously unused energies are freed in an impactful way.

Lecture III describes the neurotic as holding onto his guilt and resentment toward his parents, who were exactly what he needed and whom he can continue to blame for his problems instead of becoming self-supporting in developing his own resources. One of the most effective ways of finding what parts of the person are disowned or projected is by exploring his dreams. Gestalt therapy approaches dreams by having the person play all parts of the dream, both persons and objects, and then helping him to assimilate what has been projected. The person is also instructed to examine his dream for avoidances.

Lecture IV discusses exercises that can be used for self-growth. By following procedures of mediation, by listening to ourselves, by remaining with boredom, unpleasantness, or frustration, we may be able to resolve impasses and contribute to our own development. One technique is to fantasy the presence of a therapist who is giving us help or directions. Perls also makes several suggestions for therapists, including taking their own boredom seriously and withdrawing into fantasy instead of forcing attentiveness.

The lectures are followed by four papers which discuss more fully the theoretical aspects of Gestalt therapy. Kepner and Brien attempt to reconcile the phenomenological and behavioristic positions, keeping the strengths of each. Behaviorism, by dealing with observable events, can more easily experiment with, measure, and demonstrate change. Phenomenology, with its emphasis on internal experience, includes much of what is warm, personal, important, and rich in personality. However, the internal is private and difficult to communicate. Gestalt techniques help to unite these positions, both by bringing certain behaviors into awareness and by changing internal processes and fantasies into overt behavior.

"Present-centeredness in Gestalt Therapy" (Naranjo) undertakes an extensive exploration of the meaning of *now* in Gestalt theory and practice. Naranjo summarizes the underlying principles of Gestalt therapy and condenses them into three general processes: living in the present, awareness, and responsibility. In focusing on the implications of living in the present, he turns first to the Gestalt techniques of translating fantasies and memories into the present and of experimenting with the awareness continuum. He parallels the patient's attempt to focus and report on his present awarenesses with the Eastern process of meditation; this attempt is shared with the therapist whose presence sharpens awareness, enhances attention and meaning, adds interpersonal content, and points up difficulties. The therapist is also able to monitor errors and wanderings of attention. The Gestalt emphasis on present-centeredness is also a prescription for the good life. Many therapy techniques, such as expressing aggression and being honest, can be applied only with caution to living in the broader community. However, the prescription to live in the present is applicable to living in general, resulting in a humanistic hedonism in which an awareness of transitoriness and death sharpens the experience of living. Presentness is shown as an ideal, a sign of optimal living, akin to that described by Oriental sages, Western philosophers, and poets. It represents an acceptance of one's experiences, of the goodness of the world, and of the impossibility of living other than in the here and now.

"Sensory Functioning in Psychotherapy" (Polster) emphasizes the union or conjunction between sensory and motor functioning, or awareness and expression. Experiences may be described as *cumulative*, that is, as a total or unified event, or as *ingredient*, in which one aspect of an event is focused on. Often, when the ingredient experiences are explored by a process of analysis and resynthesis, the cumulative experience may be heightened. To reexperience and recover sensation requires effort and concentration. Polster describes ways of identifying and activating sensation and relevance of these procedures to therapy.

"The Paradoxical Theory of Change" (Beisser) deals with the finding in Gestalt therapy that change occurs when one becomes what he is, not when he tries to become what he is not. It is by not struggling against one's resistance and wish to be something else, and by recognizing oneself to be as one is, that the underlying need or wish may be recognized, the Gestalt completed, and new needs and behaviors can emerge. Beisser notes that since society continues to change in an accelerating pattern, therapy cannot prepare man to deal with a static or constant world, hence the ability to produce change becomes increasingly important.

Just as new techniques are constantly being devised by therapists as they respond to the needs of a patient in the therapeutic situation, so applications of Gestalt theory and techniques are being increasingly extended to many problems and situations that differ from the more narrowly defined therapeutic endeavor. Gestalt therapists may use their skills in such areas as the crises of normal college students, visual problems, and awareness training of professional groups. Persons with special skills in other fields may combine these with Gestalt techniques, resulting in productive combinations such as art therapy. Gestalt approaches may be used in a classroom for disturbed children or in a day-care center. In the last essay, "Person, Dialogue, and the Organismic Event: A Point of View Regarding Crisis Psychotherapy" O'Connell writes a poetic account of crisis experiences in "normal" college students. He views crises as points at which a person is called on to make a step forward in his development. However, as growth often involves conflict and suffering, many will hang back and try to maintain the status quo or attempt to solve the problem "in their heads." O'Connell emphasizes the importance of the personal involvement of the therapist and the need to avoid making the student into a patient by overconcern with his symptoms rather than with his struggles. He sees crisis resolution as first dealing with the actual environmental pressures and then utilizing other environmental supports. When the environmental pressures have been reduced, the student can focus on the internal changes necessary. Final resolution occurs in four steps: allowing oneself to be processed, saying good-by, forgiveness, and allowing oneself to love.

1
GESTALT THERAPY AND GESTALT PSYCHOLOGY*

Richard Wallen

Gestalt therapy has been nourished from all the main lines of theoretical development that have branched from the original psychoanalytic movement. It is not oriented exclusively to Gestalt psychology. Although it has important roots there, it also has roots with the Freudian psychoanalytic movement, with Otto Rank, and with Wilhelm Reich. The concept that unifies these varied approaches, which gives a rationale to the techniques employed in Gestalt therapy, is the conception of the need-fulfillment pattern in the individual as a process of Gestalt formation and destruction. I shall talk about this first. Then I shall show the ways this process is interfered with and the implications of the interference for neurotic behavior and for therapeutic technique.

The academic Gestalt psychologist dealt largely with external figures, notably visual and auditory. Interestingly enough, the academic Gestalt psychologist

* Paper presented at the Ohio Psychological Association Meeting, 1957. It is reprinted here through the courtesy of the Gestalt Institute of Cleveland, which has distributed copies upon request.

never attempted to employ the various principles of gestalt formation (proximity, the law of good continuation, *pregnanz*, similarity, and so on) to organic perceptions, to the perception of one's own feelings, emotions, and bodily sensations. He never really managed to integrate the facts of motivation with the facts of perception. It is this additional importation into Gestalt psychology that Frederick Perls made. Thus we can now conceptualize the process by which the organism finds its satisfactions in the environment as essentially that of a gestalt formation, in which there are a number of subwholes—certain subsidiary formations. To the external perceptions that the Gestalt psychologists Wertheimer and Kohler studied, the Gestalt therapist adds the figural perception of the *Gestalten* that form in the body and in the relationship of the individual to the environment.

Consider a person sitting alone reading. The book holds the center of his interest: All the rest of the room has become background; in fact his body also has become background. It is not even correct to say that he is conscious or aware of this particular reading process: he is just engaged, in contact with the ideas. Suppose that in the midst of this reading, he gets progressively thirstier. What happens is that the mouth and the inside of the mouth become figural and soon dominate the field. The book moves into the background, and the person feels something akin to "I am thirsty!" He becomes aware, in other words, of a change in himself that has implications for his relationship to the external environment. His need tends to organize both the perceptual qualities of his own experience and his motor behavior. He may have a visual image of a faucet or a glass of water or a can of beer in the icebox. He gets up, walks, satisfies the thirst, and comes back to the reading. Once more, the ideas become figural; thirst has been destroyed.

In this simple model we have the prototype of gestalt formation and destruction. The phenomenal world is organized by the needs of the individual. Needs energize behavior and organize it on the subjective-perceptual level and on the objective-motor level. The individual then carries out the necessary activities in order to satisfy the needs. After satisfaction, the mouth recedes into the background, the concern with the particular figure of water or beer disappears, and something new emerges. We have a hierarchy of needs continually developing, organizing the figures of experience, and disappearing. We describe this process in Gestalt therapy as progressive formation and destruction of perceptual and motor gestalts.

When this process is going well, when it is well integrated—when the *Gestalten* are what the academic psychologist would call firm, or strong, or well formed—certain kinds of conditions can be reported by the individual himself or can be observed by an outside observer. For one thing, figure and ground become sharply differentiated. There is no longer a cluttered field, but rather one thing that draws the individual's attention. His perceptual activity becomes selective as he becomes concerned with this particular thing. The motor behavior too becomes well organized, unified, coherent, and directed toward the satisfaction of this particular need. Similarly, the figures that the individual experiences are unitary, they cohere, and they dominate his phenomenal field.

The interesting thing about this experience from

the standpoint of adjustment is that this process of gestalt formation and destruction can provide an autonomous criterion for adjustment. In other words it is immaterial whether the individual is "mature" or "immature" by some cultural standard, or whether he conforms to society or not. The important thing from the Gestalt viewpoint is that the integrated individual is a person in whom this process is going on constantly without interruption. New figures are continually being formed. When the needs are satisfied, these figures are destroyed and replaced by others, permitting the needs next highest in the dominance hierarchy to organize behavior and perceptual experience. This process is of considerable interest because it never stops, and the Gestalt therapist can determine how well the process is going at each moment in the work he does. In the therapeutic session, the therapist can see the individual experiencing certain needs, trying to fulfill them but failing because the process is interrupted somehow or is cluttered up. This is not something that you have to talk about in the past tense. The individual's typical methods of gestalt formation and destruction are immediately apparent in the therapeutic session.

The importance of this process for biological survival should be evident, for only as the individual is able to extract from the environment those things that he needs in order to survive, in order to feel comfortable and interested in the world around him, will he actually be able to live on both a biological and psychological level. We cannot feed off ourselves; we cannot breathe without breathing in the environment; we cannot do anything to take into our bodies those necessary things that we require, whether it is affection, knowledge, or air, without interacting with the environment. Consequently, the clarity of this relationship that I have tried to describe, gestalt formation and destruction, becomes of the utmost importance for the individual's living.

What is it that causes this process to fail? Why is it that the process of progressive formation and destruction of strong *Gestalten* actually does not run its appropriate course for the individual? First, let me point out the signs that can be observed when this process is interfered with. There are subjective signs that can be reported by the patient and there are signs the therapist can see. An example of a subjective sign would be confusion: the patient feels confused and nothing stands out clearly to him. He doesn't know what he wants. He doesn't know what is important. Or, he may say that he is undecided; he doesn't know which of various alternatives to take—nothing draws him more than anything else. On the objective side, the therapist can see fixed and repetitive behavior. For example, we see a patient ask for advice again and again or ask for instructions when told to explore and find his own answers. The whole self-regulation of the environment-organism relationship is destroyed. Also noticeable is the patient's lack of interest in what he himself is doing, and consequently the feeling of great effort in connection with some simple task. Patients report: "I have to force myself to go to work"; "I have to force myself to study"; and so on. Speech is usually poorly organized, and there will be actual confusion in what the patient says. Sometimes these things may be only momentary; at other times they may last for a substantial period of time.

It is important, however, to remember that a field

that is poorly organized is still organized. The principle of *pregnanz* points out that any psychological field is as well organized as the global conditions will permit at that particular time. So it is possible, as was recognized by Koffka and Kohler years ago, that certain circumstances can prevent a figure from forming itself into the strongest and most coherent possible figure. In neurotic self-regulation certain forces are impeded from exerting their full effect on organismic contact with the environment. These interferences are of three kinds:

First, there is poor perceptual contact with the external world and with the body itself. We notice, for example, that patients will often not look at us when they are trying to tell us something about how we impressed them; or they will not look at objects that they are trying to describe. They may be unable to notice what they themselves are doing with their hands; or they do not hear the sound of their own voices, and so on. Their perceptual contact with large parts of their environment and of their bodies is either poor or blocked completely.

Second, the open expression of needs is blocked. For example, the patient may feel some warmth but not be able to do anything about it. One can see why this would result in a failure of the destructive process. Since the patient does not express his needs, he actually never gets the satisfaction for them; a perceptual figure that could have been bright, unified, and meaningful becomes dull and uninteresting, and the need thus actually never gets discharged. For example, consider somebody with a need for affection that is only half expressed. Half satisfaction results because the need is never thoroughly discharged.

This particular need then serves to energize parts of the perceptual field: the person is looking for affection but not really wholeheartedly. The end result is that the need continues interfering with other kinds of needs that might organize the field in a clear-cut and coherent way.

Third, repression can prevent the formation of good *Gestalten*. The Gestalt therapist's view of repression as essentially a motor process is rather surprising from a historical point of view because the academic Gestalt psychologist was not concerned with what the musculature was doing, what the total gestalt formation would be like in, for example, walking. Largely because of the influence of Wilhelm Reich, Gestalt therapists consider repression as essentially a muscular phenomenon. Thus when needs and impulses arise, there tends to be a muscular response. The response tends to play itself out on the motor level, and the only way that one can inhibit the response is by contracting antagonistic muscles that prevent his impulse from expressing itself fully. The simplest example would be an impulse to swear at somebody. Let us suppose that you are very angry and yet you have to hold the impulse back. Now this "holding back" process can be seen as a strictly muscular process. There are contractions in the jaws; there are tensions in the arm that prevent, for example, shaking the fist. In the case of sadness, the normal postural responses if the need played itself out thoroughly would be dejected posture, drawn mouth, and empty face. In holding sadness back, the simplest alteration would be to push the lips upward into a smile, destroying the pattern associated with sadness and thus not expressing and discharging the emotion.

In repression all sorts of impulse unawareness are maintained by chronic muscular contractions which are forgotten by the individual. They become habitual; the individual adapts to them and does not know that he is blocking something or what it is that he is blocking.

What are some of the implications for therapy? It seems to me that one of the most distinctive things about the Gestalt therapist is that he works almost exclusively in the present. He is not primarily concerned with the recovery of past memories. The past has some importance in certain special circumstances, but, by and large, the Gestalt therapist sees that the only thing he has to work with is that which is immediately in front of him. In the therapeutic session itself the process of gestalt formation and destruction goes on as it does anywhere. The therapist has an opportunity to see the confusions that arise. He can see how the patient blocks out portions of his environment or portions of himself. Thus, the therapist begins to work with this particular problem.

At this point it is only fair to say that this approach to the therapy process represents one of the great streams of psychotherapeutic thought that stems from Otto Rank, who influenced Carl Rogers' client-centered therapy in a somewhat different way. Rogers' followers were interested in the present situation, too. They also focused on what the client was doing, but they never did get to the problem of the real *awareness* of what was happening to the patient *at this instant*. There is a great tendency, it seems to me, for words to get in the way of experience, and the Gestalt psychologists have tried to remedy this. This is not to say that there are not very strong Gestalt implications in Rogers' client-centered therapy, as he himself has pointed out, but the Gestalt therapist is basically much more active than the Rogerian therapist.

What is the therapist's activity directed toward? First, to break up the patient's chronically poorly organized field. The patient has certain standard ways of perceiving or acting in relationship to a need. The Gestalt therapist isolates portions of this field so that the self-regulating tendency of the neurotic can be broken up into smaller subunits. This eventually will permit the reorganization of both the motor field and the perceptual field. Also the Gestalt therapist works to heighten each emerging figure. If the patient seems ready to cry, for example, if there is an emerging activity the therapist can see "on the surface," if he notices squeezing and contractions in the face and perhaps a glistening of the eyes, he knows that the figure of crying is emerging. Suppose, however, that the impulse is being held back by the patient. The therapist works to unblock the impulse so that it can organize the field. He may do this by taking the resistance, the muscular resistance to crying, as the figure of the patient's attention. In other words, instead of emphasizing "You want to cry," he emphasizes "*How* are you preventing yourself from crying?" He goes back over and over again to the problem of "what are you doing that prevents you from getting what you want at this moment, in this immediate situation?" This means, of course, that there must be a great deal of bodily sensitivity, so a large part of the therapist's activity is devoted to body awareness. Until the patient can *feel* how he contracts his muscles or how he manipulates his head or his eyes or his body in order to prevent himself from seeing or doing certain things, he cannot make the repressive mechanism a matter of choice. It is not that we want to destroy his ability to control himself, but rather that we want to make it a matter of intentional choice.

These then are the major theoretical issues which form the broad base on which the Gestalt therapist works. This approach represents an extension of academic Gestalt psychology by adding needs and bodily awareness to the gestalt-forming process and then utilizing these insights in therapy to help unblock the need-fulfillment pattern.

2
FOUR LECTURES[*]

Frederick S. Perls

I

In my lectures in Gestalt therapy, I have one aim only: to impart a fraction of the meaning of the word *now*. To me, nothing exists except the now. Now = experience = awareness = reality. The past is no more and the future not yet. Only the *now* exists.

The plight of the psychology of our time is that we are basically divided into two classes: the one interested in behavior and the other interested in awareness, or lack of awareness—be it called consciousness, experience, or whatever. This is the phenomenological approach which emphasizes the messages that are self-evident—existential in the pure sense—that we receive through the organs of our senses. We know through seeing, hearing, feeling; from these come the primary information we get about ourselves and our relation to life. The behaviorist, on the other hand, is not interested in the phenomenon of awareness and the subjective approach. He does, however, have the great advantage over most other methods in that he works in the

[*] Transcribed from talks given at the Atlanta Workshop in Gestalt Therapy, 1966.

here and now. He sees *this* animal, looks at *this* person, and investigates how *this* person is behaving. If you put these two together—the phenomenological approach, the awareness of what is, and the behavioral approach with its emphasis on behavior in the now—then you have in a nutshell what we are trying to do in Gestalt therapy.

When we look at behavior, we see essentially two kinds: public behavior and private behavior. Public behavior is overt observable behavior of which observers and we ourselves may be aware, and private behavior includes those things of which we may be aware, but an observer is not. This private behavior is usually called thinking, or speculating, or rehearsing, or computing.

Before I go any further, I would like to discuss briefly four basic philosophical approaches, as I see them. The first approach is *science,* or as I call it, "aboutism," which lets us talk *about* things, gossip *about* ourselves or others, broadcast *about* what's going on in ourselves, talk *about* our cases. Talking about things, or ourselves and others as though we were things, keeps out any emotional responses or other genuine involvement. In therapy, aboutism is found in rationalization and intellectualization, and in the "interpretation game" where the therapist says, "This is what your difficulties are *about.*" This approach is based on noninvolvement.

The second philosophy I call "shouldism." The "should" mentality is found overtly or covertly in every philosophy and definitely in every religion. Even in Buddhism there is an implied shouldism, in that you *should* experience Nirvana, you *should* achieve the state of freedom from suffering; at least it is praised as something worth achieving. Religions are full of taboos, of *shoulds* and *should nots*. I'm sure you all realize that you grow up completely surrounded by what you should and should not do, and that you spend much of your time playing this game within yourself—the game I call the "top-dog/under-dog game," or the "self-improvement game," or the "self-torture game." I'm certain that you are very familiar with this game. One part of you talks to the other part and says, "You should be better, you should not be this way, you should not do that, you shouldn't be what you are, you should be what you are not." Shouldism is based on the phenomenon of dissatisfaction.

Lately a third kind of thinking has come about: ontological thinking, or the existential approach, or "is-ism." This looks at and perceives the world as it *is*, as we *are*, making irrelevant and bracketing off what we *should* be. You might call this the eternal attempt to achieve truth. But what is truth? Truth is one of what I call the "fitting games."

Here I will wander off a minute and talk about some of the important games. One of the main games we play is the "one-upmanship game": "I'm better than you are," "I can trump you," "I can depress you." A second main game is the "fitting game": "Does this concept *fit* reality?" "Is this correct?" "If I see this and this, can I fit them together so that I can see a comprehensive picture?" "Does the behavior of this person fit into my concept of how a person should behave?" These are some of the fitting games. Now in existentialism the fitting game is truth. By "truth" I mean nothing but the assertion that a statement we make fits the observable reality. If a person says, "I'm angry with you," in a soft, polite tone of voice, it doesn't fit. His tone of voice is inconsistent with the anger he claims to feel. If he says, "Damn you! I'm angry with you!" then his anger and voice fit.

But none of the existentialists, with the possible exception of Heidegger, can really carry through their existential idea to ontological behavior—that a thing is explained through its very existence. They keep asking "Why?" and so have to keep going back and getting support: Sartre from Communism, Buber from Judaism, Tillich from Protestantism, Heidegger to a small extent from Nazism, Binswanger from psychoanalysis. Binswanger in particular is always trying to go back to the causal—to that semantic mistake—trying to explain the event by its precedent, by its history, and therefore making the usual mistake of mixing up memories and history.

Finally, there is the Gestalt approach, which attempts to understand the existence of any event through the way it comes about, which tries to understand becoming by the *how*, not the *why*; through the all pervasive gestalt formation; through the tension of the unfinished situation, which is the biological factor. In other words, in Gestalt therapy we try to be consistent with every other event, especially with nature because we are a part of nature. That our life is not consistent with the demands of society is not because nature is at fault or we are at fault, but because society has undergone a process that has moved it so far from healthy functioning, natural functioning, that our needs and the needs of society and the needs of nature do not fit together any more. Again and again we come into such conflict until it becomes doubtful whether a healthy and fully sane and honest person can exist in our insane society.

Now, I would like to discuss what I think are the two most important discoveries of Freud. Freud said (this is not his formulation, but my understanding of what he meant) that in a neurosis a part of our personality or of our potential is not available. But he said this in an odd way; he said, "it is *in* the unconscious," as if there were such a thing as *the* unconscious rather than simply behavior or emotions that are unknown or not available. Freud also saw the basis of the gestalt formation in what he called the "preconscious." We call it the "background" out of which the figure emerges. We can go further and point up the fact that only a small portion of our potential—of what we could be—is available.

The other important discovery of Freud, which he never followed up and which seems to have gotten lost, is his remark, "*Denken ist Probearbeit*" ("Thinking is trial work"). I have reformulated it this way, "Thinking is rehearsing." Thinking is rehearsing in fantasy for the role you have to play in society. And when it comes to the moment of performance, and you're not sure whether your performance will be well received, then you get stage fright. This stage fright has been given by psychiatry the name "*anxiety*." "What will I have to say on the examination?" "What will I say in my lecture?" You meet a girl and think "What will I have to wear to impress her?" and so on. All of this is rehearsing for the role you play. I think Freud's sentence "*Denken ist Probearbeit*" is one of his great ideas.

Part of the reason why Freud could not follow up

this idea was because rehearsing is relating to the future, and Freud was concerned only with the past. So this concept did not fit into his general theory and he had to drop it. But I would like you to consider for a moment how much time and how much of your potential you invest in thinking or rehearsing for the future in comparison with how much time you invest in thinking about the past.

Now, I can again talk about the *now*.

I maintain that all therapy that has to be done can only be done in the now. Anything else is interfering. And the technique that lets us understand and stay with the now is the "awareness continuum," discovering and becoming fully aware of each actual experience. If you can stay with this, you will soon come across some experience which is unpleasant. For instance, you get bored, or feel uncomfortable, or feel like crying. At that moment, something happens which Freud did not see clearly enough; at that point we become phobic. Freud saw the active blocking out of experience and called it "repression." He also saw the alienation of our experience and called it "projection." What I want to point out is that the critical moment is the frequent interruption of whatever we experience in the now. We interrupt by various means: we start to explain, we suddenly discover that we have taken up too much of the group's time, we remember that we have something important to do, or we get into the schizophrenic flight of ideas which is called by psychoanalysis "free association" (even though it is compulsive dis-association). This interruption of the awareness continuum prevents maturation, prevents therapy from becoming successful, prevents marriage from becoming richer and deeper, prevents inner conflicts from being solved. The whole purpose of this avoidance tendency is to maintain the status quo.

And what is the status quo? The status quo is *holding onto the concept that we are children.* This is opposite to the psychoanalytic viewpoint. Freud thought we are infantile because of prior trauma, but this is backward rationalization. We are infantile because we are afraid to take responsibility in the now. To take our place in history, to be mature, means giving up the concept that we have parents, that we have to be submissive or defiant, or the other variations on the child's role that we play.

In order to extend this, I need to talk about maturing. Maturation is the development from environmental support to self-support. The baby is entirely dependent on environmental support. As the child grows up, it learns more and more to stand on its own feet, create its own world, earn its own money, become emotionally independent. But in the neurotic this process does not adequately take place. The child—or the childish neurotic—will use his potential not for self-support but to act out phony roles. These phony roles are meant to mobilize the environment for support instead of mobilizing one's own potential. We manipulate the environment by being helpless, by playing stupid, asking questions, wheedling, flattering.

The result is that in life, and especially in therapy, we come to the "sick point" (as Russian psychiatry calls it), to the point where we are stuck, to the impasse. The impasse occurs where we cannot produce our own support and where environmental support is not forthcoming. In Gestalt therapy we see this happening again and again and again. Psychoanalysis unfortunately tends to foster childishness and dependency, first by its fantasies that the patient is a child and that everything should be related to a "father image" or "childhood trauma" or "transference"; and then by giving environmental support again and again in the form of intellectual interpretation which says, "I know you are stupid and immature. I know what you are doing. I know more than you. I will explain everything." But this prevents the person from truly understanding himself.

This is why I am absolutely dogmatic in regard to the fact that nothing exists except in the now, and that in the now you are behaving in a certain way that will or will not facilitate your development, your acquisition of a better ability to cope with life, to make available what was unavailable before, to begin to fill in the voids in your existence. Everyone has to some extent the kind of voids that are so apparent in the neurotic and schizophrenic. One person has no eyes, another no ears, another no legs to stand on, another no perspective, another no emotion. In order to fill these voids, which are usually experienced as boredom with life, emptiness, loneliness, we have to get through the impasse and through the frustrations of the impasse, which usually lead us to shortcut the frustrations and with them the whole learning process.

Now there are two ways of learning. In the first, you get information; you get someone to tell what your dreams mean, what concepts will be useful, what the world is like. Then you feed this into your computer and you play the fitting game. Does this concept fit in with these other concepts? However, the best way of learning is not the computation of information. Learning is discovering, uncovering what is there. When we discover, we are uncovering our own ability, our own eyes, in order to find our potential, to see what is going on, to discover how we can enlarge our lives, to find means at our disposal that will let us cope with a difficult situation. And all this, I maintain, is taking place in the here and now. Any speculation about things, any attempt at getting information and assistance from outside help will not produce maturation. So anyone who works with me has to do it with a continuous account of the now. "I am experiencing this; now I feel this; now I don't want to work anymore; now I am bored." From here we can go on to differentiate what of the now experience is acceptable to you, when you want to run away, when you are willing to suffer yourself, when you feel yourself being suffered, and so on. All of this is explored in reality, in our encounter here with each other.

Said in another way, most psychotherapies are trying to get to the deepest depth. We are trying to get to the outermost surface. As every need, every unfinished situation emerges, we are being controlled by this emergent need and have to get in touch with the world to satisfy this need. We use our senses to observe, to see what is going on. The world is opening up. This ability to see is health. Conversely, the neurotic can be defined as a person who can't see the obvious, as in Anderson's fairy tale where only the child points to the obvious—that the king is naked. This is why, when I start working with a group, I often play schoolteacher and ask them to discover and verbalize the obvious.

II

In addition to the now, I also emphasize the process of *centering*, the reconciliation of opposites so that they no longer waste energy in useless struggle with each other, but can join in productive combination and interplay. For example, let us look at one of the main problems that people think they have—the problem of their own existence.

What is the opposite of existence? The immediate answer would be nonexistence, but this is incorrect. The opposite would be antiexistence, just as the opposite of matter is antimatter. As you know, scientists have managed to create matter out of energy. What has this to do with us in psychology? Mainly that in science we have finally come back to the pre-Socratic philosopher, Heraclitus, who said that everything is flow, flux, process. There are no "things." *Nothingness* in the Eastern languages is *no-thingness*. We in the West think of nothingness as a void, an emptiness, a nonexistence. In Eastern philosophy and modern physical science, nothingness—no-thingness—is a form of process, ever moving.

In science we try to find ultimate matter, but the more we split up matter, the more we find other matter. We find movement, and movement equals energy: movement, impact, energy, but no things. Things came about, more or less, by man's need for security. You can manipulate a thing, you can play fitting games with it. These concepts, these somethings can be put together into something else. "Something" is a thing, so even an abstract noun becomes a thing.

When we work in therapy, we always come across the nothingness, and we see that this no-thingness is some very alive process. I hope you understand the meaning of dealing with things—that in order to bring things back to life, we have to change them into process again. Reification, the making a thing out of a process, is the functioning of what I call the implosive or catatonic or death layer. If you *have* a body, if you *have* a mind, these *things* are apparently objects that belong to some instance called "I." "I" am the proud possessor—or the despising possessor—of a mind, of a body, of a world. So in effect I say, "I *have* some body" (*some* body) rather than realize that I *am* somebody.

In Gestalt therapy we look at the way a person manipulates his language, and we see that the more alienated he is from himself, the more he will use nouns instead of verbs, and most especially, the word *it*. *It* is a "thing" that is convenient to use to avoid being alive. When I'm alive, I talk, I am "voicing." When I'm dead, I "have" a *voice* with *words;* this *language* will have an *expression;* etc. You notice that this description is mostly a string of nouns, and that all that remains of life is to put them together.

To help you understand the importance of the implosive layer and its role in neuroses, I will describe more completely what I consider the five layers of neurosis. The first layer we encounter is what I call the Eric Berne layer, or the Sigmund Freud layer, or the phony layer, where we play games, play roles. It is identical with Helene Deutsch's description of the "as if" person. We behave *as if* we are big shots, *as if* we are nincompoops, *as if* we are pupils, *as if* we are ladies, *as if* we are bitches, etc. It is always the "as if" attitudes that require that we live up to a concept, live up to a fantasy that we or others have created whether it comes out as a curse or as an ideal. What you call an ideal, I call a curse. It's an attempt to get away from oneself. The result is that the neurotic person has given up living for his self in a way that would actualize himself. He wants to live instead for a concept, for the actualization of this concept—like an elephant who had rather be a rose bush, and a rose bush that tries to be a kangaroo. We don't want to be ourselves; we don't want to be what we are. We want to be something else, and the existential basis of this being something else is the experience of dissatisfaction. We are dissatisfied with what we do, or parents are dissatisfied with what their child is doing. He should be different, he shouldn't be what he is; he should be something else.

Then comes religion, philosophy, the violin and strings—we should be wonderful and beautiful, and if you are a Christian, you should be unsubstantial. In the New Testament nature doesn't count: only the supernatural, miraculous counts. So there should be no substance. And if you are dead, you should not be dead. Everything is regarded as if it should not exist as it is. In other words, the constitution with which we are born—our inheritance—is despised. We are not allowed to be at home in ourselves, so we alienate those frowned-upon properties and create the holes I spoke of in my first talk, the voids, the nothingness where something should exist. And where there is something missing, we build up a phony artifact. We behave as if we actually have this property that is demanded by society and which finally comes to be demanded by what Freud called the superego, the conscience. This we encounter as the top-dog in those games that torture the under-dog, the other part of the self, by demanding the impossible—"Come on now, live up to that ideal!"

It would be nice if we could be such wonderful people, but Freud neglected an important element which we have to add. The superego is not opposed, as Freud thought, to an ego or to an id, or to a cluster of our impulses and memories and energies. The top-dog is opposed to another personality, which I call the under-dog. Both have their characteristics and both fight for control. The top-dog is characterized mainly by righteousness. Whether he is right or wrong, he always knows what the under-dog should do. But the top-dog has very few means by which to reinforce his demands. He is really just a bully and tries to get his way by making threats. If you don't do as he says, then you will be punished, or something terrible will happen. The under-dog who receives these orders is not righteous; on the contrary, he is very unsure of himself. He does not fight back or try to control by being a bully or by being aggressive. He fights back with other means. "Tomorrow." "I promise." "Yes, but . . ." "I do my best." So these two, the top-dog and the under-dog, live a life of mutual frustration and continued attempts to control each other.

This, then, is what I call the first, or phony, layer, which includes these roles, the top-dog/under-dog games, the controlling games. If we once become aware of the phoniness of game-playing and try to become more honest or genuine, then we encounter pain, unpleasantness, despair, etc. We especially don't like experiencing cruelty. "We shouldn't hurt our neighbors or anyone else." We completely forget that a basic law of nature is to kill in order to live.

There is no creature, no organic substance that can sustain its life without killing other animals or plants. Of all the species, only the human being refuses to accept the need for killing and turns killing against himself: only the human being kills not for necessity but for greed and power. Especially now, as the individual is superseded by the superorganisms called states or nations, he is deprived of his need to kill and has surrendered his needs to kill to the state.

Killing and destroying get all mixed up. Actually, we can't even eat an apple without destroying the substance of the apple. We destructure the apple as a single unit, cutting it to pieces with our front teeth, grinding it down with our back teeth, dissolving it chemically until nothing of the apple is left except substances we can't assimilate, and so eliminate.

Once we are capable of understanding our reluctance to accept unpleasant experiences, we can get to the next layer, the phobic layer, the resistance, the objection to being what we are. This is where all the *should nots* that I have already discussed occur.

If we get behind the phobic layer, the objections, we find at that moment the impasse occurs. And within the impasse there is the feeling of being not alive, of deadness. We feel that we are nothing, we are things. In every bit of therapy we have to go through this implosive layer in order to get to the authentic self. This is where most schools of therapy and therapists shrink away, because they also fear deadness. Of course, it is not being dead, but the fear and feeling of being dead, of disappearing. The fantasy is taken for reality. Once we get through the implosive layer, we see something very peculiar happening. This can be seen most dramatically in the catatonic state, when the patient who has appeared as a corpse explodes to life. And this is what happens when the implosive state is dissolved—explosions happen.

The explosion is the final neurotic layer that occurs when we get through the implosive state. As I see it, this progression is necessary to become authentic. There are essentially four types of explosion: explosion into joy, into grief, into orgasm, into anger. Sometimes the explosions are very mild—it depends on the amount of energy that has been invested in the implosive layer.

Perhaps I can make clearer where the catatonic state, the implosive state, comes about by talking about physiology. You know that in order to move a muscle, you send an electric shock into the muscle, and the muscle jerks. If you interrupt the shock, again the muscle jerks. In order to keep the muscle contracted you must constantly repeat the electric shocks. So you can imagine in a catatonic state, or anytime you get tense, how much energy is invested in keeping tense, keeping rigid. And if this energy is not invested in keeping yourself rigid, the energy is freed for all kinds of activities—thinking, moving about, being alive. If suddenly freed, the pent-up energy will explode. Implosion becomes explosion, compression becomes expression.

I think I will give the group now a few minutes for questions and remarks about this lecture.

Question: You mentioned that getting through the implosive layer to the explosion may be perceived by both the patient and therapist as dangerous, and probably that's the reason for the implosive layer. How do the therapist and the patient get beyond this? I have a patient that has exploded from a catatonic state into orgasm, and it looks like he may go back to the implosive layer or to catatonia because he can't adjust either way.

Perls: One thing you have to remember is that a person, in order to function well, has to have all four abilities for explosion available. The person who can explode into orgasm, but not anger or grief or joy is incomplete. What you're talking about is what I mentioned as the phobic layer avoiding the experience of the tension because of catastrophic fantasies, the fear of the risk. When so much energy is held back, so much life energy or *elan vital* is accumulated that the person can't hold it back any longer and the explosion may occur in a very violent way.

Comment: It reminds me of the explosion when atoms are separated—fission.

Perls: Fusion or fission. There is one way where the explosion and the danger of explosion is often diminished. This is the process of melting. Often you will find that at a certain point you are moved, you are involved, and you begin to melt, you feel soft, or you begin to cry. This is one of the buffers against a dangerous explosion. But basically one has to be willing to take risks.

Question: Is melting tenderness?

Perls: Tenderness is a form of melting. You will find that after a good explosion you will feel tender in the meaning of being subtle. But when you talk about tenderness, I am suspicious. It sounds like the undercore of toughness, and playing the toughy is a very important part of role-playing for the American youth.

Question: Would you say a bit about that—about youth playing the role of toughness?

Perls: Where does the American child get a great part of his information? From the comic strips. And what do the comic strips say? Do they talk about a man and a woman? No. They deal with the he-man and the glamour girl. This concept of a man is more like a cave man than a genuine man—and this is difficult to define—a man in the sense of living for his convictions. But the comic-strip message is that a man has to be a toughy because otherwise he's a sissy. He has no other choice except to become a baseball hero or a homosexual. Only as a homosexual is he allowed to be tender, to be soft. The same is true for the female. A rough estimate is that the American female is divided into 90 percent bitches and 10 percent women. Women have to become bitches because they have to become glamour girls. As glamour girls they have to spend most of their time being photogenic and being looked at instead of having eyes, having genitals, having relationships. This results in a permanent kind of irritation, a permanent hostility. The man is seen as the enemy, and the only way to keep the enemy under control is to become a bitch. So the he-man and the bitch fit together as the main characters on the American stage.

Question: I only heard you mention four of the layers of neurosis.

Perls: The phony layer, the phobic, the impasse, the implosive, the explosive. If I categorize in this way and make a thing out of a process, please be tolerant and see that this is just an approximation of what the process is like.

Question: The phony level is where the games go on?

Perls: Yes.

Question: And the implosive layer is where the reasons for the games are. Is this right?

Perls: No. There are no reasons for the games.

Comment: Then I don't understand the implosive layer.

Perls: The implosive level is where the energies that are needed for living are frozen and invested unused. In order to free them for living we have to go through the process of exploding. If I'm thirsty, I do not have to go into the woods and find a spring with water. This would be the biological, primitive way. In our culture, I have to use a number of manipulations. For example, at this conference I ring a bell, and give the waiter orders, and go through all kinds of processes so that I can get water to balance out the minus in my organism. In the culture in which we live, we have to play roles in order to satisfy our needs. Now I could conceivably go into the corridor and explode. *"Hello, hello! I want something to drink!"* But I don't do this. I play the prescribed roles. I'm polite and considerate.

Question: Will you say some more about the phobic layer?

Perls: The main phobic attitude I can think of is being phobic about discovering life. In order to avoid living a life of discovering the world and ourselves, we often take the short-cut of getting information. This is what you did right now—you asked me for information. But you could have set out and discovered what you are phobic about or what somebody else is phobic about—what you or they avoid. But instead you ask me to feed your computer, your thinking system. The basic phobic attitude is to be afraid to be what you are. And you will find relief immediately if you dare to investigate what you are like. You'll find that immediately you run into catastrophic fantasies. "If I am as I am, what will happen to me? Society will ostracize me. If I tell my boss to go to hell, I'll lose my job. If I tell my wife she's a bitch, she won't sleep with me." And so on and so on. So you become phobic, you start to manipulate, to play roles. Instead of saying, "You're a bitch," you compress your lips and don't talk to her. But you contract yourself and signal indirectly that you don't like what she's doing or the way she is. You *im*plode yourself, because you are afraid to *ex*plode.

Question: When one is at the impasse level, is one afraid to see the world for what it is?

Perls: No, there is more to it. The impasse occurs every time you are not ready or willing to use your own resources (including your eyes) and when environmental support is not forthcoming. The extreme example of the impasse is the blue baby. The blue baby cannot provide its own oxygen, and the mother doesn't provide oxygen any more. The blue baby is at an impasse of breathing, and he has to find a way to breathe or die. Another good example of impasse is the average marriage, where the two partners are not in love with each other but with a concept of what the other should be. Each has almost no idea of what the other is like, and as soon as the behavior of one doesn't fit with what the partner expects, he becomes dissatisfied and starts playing the blaming game. He blames her: she should change; he blames himself: he should change —all this rather than realize that they are in an impasse because they are in love with an image, a fantasy. They are stuck. But they don't know *how* they are stuck, and that's the impasse. The result of the impasse is to keep the status quo. They may want to change, but they dont: they keep the status quo because they are too frightened of going through the impasse.

Question: What breaks the impasse?
Perls: The impasse cannot be broken.
Question: It has to be accepted?
Perls: You might say that. The incredible thing which is so difficult to understand is that experience, awareness of the now, is sufficient to solve all difficulties of this nature, that is, neurotic difficulties. If you are fully aware of the impasse, the impasse will collapse, and you will find yourself suddenly through it. I know this sounds rather mystical, so I will give you an example. There are two items on the menu and you cannot decide which to order. But nature does not work by decisions but by preferences. If you prefer one food more than the other, you are through the impasse.

III

There are three themes I would like to touch on now. The first is the matter of answering patients' questions. You may have wondered about the fact that I almost never answer questions during therapy. Instead I usually ask the patient to change the question into a statement. The question mark has a hook the patient may use for many purposes, such as to embarrass the other person or, more often, to prevent himself from discovering what is really going on. This asking for environmental support keeps one in the infantile state. You will find that nothing develops your intelligence better than to take any question and turn it into a genuine statement. Suddenly the background will start to open up, and the ground from which the question grows will become visible.

A second theme concerns guilt feelings. According to psychoanalytic theory, the patient is cured if he is free from anxiety and guilt. Anxiety we have already dealt with as stage fright. The problem of guilt is even simpler: *guilt is projected resentment.* Any time you feel guilty, you will find a nucleus of resentment. But resentment in itself is still an incomplete emotion. Resentment is an effort at maintaining the status quo, a hanging-on; in resentment you can neither let go and be done by giving up, nor can you be aggressive and angry and clear up the situation. Resentment is the bite that hangs on.

Possibly the most difficult mental feat for any patient is to forgive his parents. Parents are never right. They are either too stern or too soft, too strong or too weak. There is always something wrong with parents. And the balance between guilt feelings (that he owes them something) and resentment (that they owe him something) is achieved by a very peculiar phenomenon—gratefulness. Gratefulness leads to closure. Neither party owes the other anything.

My third theme is the importance of dreams. The dream is an existential message. It is more than an unfinished situation; it is more than an unfulfilled wish; it is more than a prophecy. It is a message of yourself to yourself, to whatever part of you is listening. The dream is possibly the most spontaneous expression of the human being, a piece of art that we chisel out of our lives. And every part, every situation in the dream is a creation of the dreamer himself. Of course, some of the pieces come from memory or reality, but the important question is what makes the dreamer pick out this specific piece? No choice in the dream is coincidental. As in paranoia, the person who is projecting looks for a peg on which to hang his hat. Every aspect of it is a part of the dreamer, but a part that to some extent is disowned and projected onto other objects. What does projection mean? That we have disowned, alienated, certain parts of ourselves and put them out into the world rather than having them available as our own potential. We have emptied a part of ourselves into the world; therefore we must be left with holes, with emptiness. If we want to own these parts of ourselves again we have to use special techniques by which we can reassimilate those experiences.

In working with a dream, I avoid any interpretation. I leave this to the patient since I believe he knows more about himself than I can possibly know. I used to go through the whole dream and work through every part; but many patients have difficulty in reidentification, and the difficulty is absolutely identical with the amount of self-alienation. Lately I take more of a short cut. I look mainly for the holes, the emptiness, the avoidances.

The first problem, then, is to find out what the dream is avoiding. Often we are immediately able to find what the patient is avoiding by finding out at what moment he interrupts the dream and wakes up rather than continue it. Very often the dreamer is avoiding death, being killed, or sex. Actually, I find that the whole question of survival, of killing and destroying, is at least as important as the sexual question.

Question: You say when the dream is interrupted by waking, we are avoiding something, but what if it is not interrupted by waking?

Perls: Then it is not always as easy to find out what is being avoided. Usually when you allow yourself to go on dreaming, you are not trying to avoid some terrible shock, as in a dream of falling in which you have to wake before you are smashed. Evasion is the usual base of neurosis, based on a misunderstanding of fantasy and reality. I can fall a thousand times in fantasy. I can kill a hundred people in my dreams—it is only fantasy and they are still alive. It is tragic that we are so unwilling even to imagine certain situations, so this fear of imagination, this mixing up of reality and fantasy persists. We stop ourselves from doing many things because we imagine the bad things that will happen, or we feel disappointed because all the rosy things we expect and wish just do not happen. All those wonderful things—we go to Las Vegas with five dollars and come back with a hundred thousand; or we dream of being a wonderful, perfect human being. This doesn't happen, so we are disappointed. We prevent ourselves from using what we have or from reassimilating what we have disowned.

Let me give you an example. A woman dreamed that she had three orphans and each of the orphans had an artificial hand or arm, all very beautifully carved, and she was looking for the best surgeon to make the best possible prosthesis substitute for the hands. Where is the avoidance, the emptiness here? Well, it is obvious. So, I became very cruel and brutal, and took the prosthesis away from the children. The children were left without hands. Where were the hands? Obviously in the person who made the prosthesis. I learned that this woman was very artistically inclined and had sculpted for many years, but had lost the ability. So the carvings, the artistic abilities came out as a projection. The minus, the avoidance of existence in this case is the lack of organic hands. By working through this dream, I could give her back the use and appreciation of her hands.

Let me warn you to be very careful about dreams and dreamers who have no living beings in their dreams. Where there is only death or desert or buildings, you are most likely to have a severe psychotic case on your hands.

It is also important to let patients play at being the objects in the dream as well as the persons. Two of my favorite examples of this are from the same man. In one dream, he leaves my office, crosses the street into Central Park, and walks over the bridle path. I ask him to play the bridle path, and he answers, "What! And let everybody tramp and shit on me?" In another dream, he left his attache case on the stairs. I asked him to be the attache case. He said, "Well, I've got a thick hide, in a thick skin. I've got secrets and nobody is supposed to get to my secrets. I keep them absolutely safe." See how much he tells us about himself by playing, identifying with the objects in his dreams? Also, you will learn a lot by paying attention to the locale, where the dream is staged.

If a person dreams that he is in court, you know he is concerned with guilt, being accused, etc. If the dream takes place in a motel, you can guess what his existence is like.

The more you refrain from interfering and telling the patient what he is like or what he feels like, the more chance you give him to discover himself and not to be misled by your concepts and projections. And believe me, it is never easy to be able to differentiate between what we project and what we see and hear. Probably the most dangerous thing for a therapist to do is to play the computer game. You find patients whose life exists of sentences and computing, and if you feed information into their computers, and they compute back to you, nothing will *ever* happen. The computer game can go on for years and years.

To recapitulate: The two main words I want to impress on you are *now* and *how*. The difficulties lie in getting again and again pulled away from the now and into all kinds of rationalizations and making cases as to who is right and who is wrong. "I have a better interpretation than you have." "I know all about you." There is also the great danger of the Freudian approach. "This happens *because* it has happened before." As if one railroad station could be explained because there was another one before it. And you must be very careful to teach your patients to differentiate between reality and their fantasies, especially the transference fantasy—where they see you as a father or someone who can give them the goodies. Make them look again and again to see the difference between this father and you until they wake up and come to their senses.

Even if you are compulsive about *now* and *how*,

it can't do any harm, and the compulsion will dissolve into something alive and meaningful.

We don't know what the next step in history will be. We have come from the gods, to the causes of nature, to the process. Right now we live in the age of processes. I am sure that one day we will discover that awareness is a property of the universe—extension, duration, awareness. Right now the first experiments are being made. Flatworms have been cut up and fed to other worms, and experiments show that these know what the first generation had learned. Possibly this is the first step in demonstrating that awareness is a property of matter. But we cannot yet think in terms of billions and billions of parts of the quantum to measure awareness, and the idea that properties might exist that are not measurable is still beyond the concepts of today's psychologists.

Full identification with yourself can take place if you are willing to take full responsibility—*responseability*—for yourself, for your actions, feelings, thoughts; and if you stop mixing up responsibility with obligation. This is another semantic confusion in psychology. Most people believe that responsibility means, "I put myself under obligation." But it does not. You are responsible only for yourself. *I am responsible only for myself.* This is what I tell a patient right away. If he wants to commit suicide, that's his business. If he wants to go crazy, that's his business. Jewish mothers have wonderful ways of manipulating people; they are experts on making one feel guilty, on pushing the buttons of conscience. But I am not in this world to live up to other people's expectations, nor do I feel that the world must live up to mine.

Four Lectures

Question: I've been putting together a number of things that you've said, and they're making me uncomfortable. If a law of nature is to kill to maintain life, then how do we decide when transgression is harmful to ourselves, or dangerous to others, or unacceptable to them?

Perls: You want a prescription for behavior—for instance, how to make decisions. I cannot and will not provide you with that. Any decision has to be made by the situation in which an event occurs. Science has only recently proceeded from looking at pieces to recognizing the total approach, the Gestalt approach. Students have been taught that the organism consists of a number of reflex arcs, or that mind is over against matter, or that here is a person and there is the environment—not that here is a person who has accumulated some emotions that need to be relieved. I think that the Freudian "excremental" theory of emotions—that we have a certain quantum of aggression that should be discharged—is especially dangerous.

We are part of the universe, not separate. We and our environment are one. We cannot look without something to look at. We cannot breathe without air. We cannot live without being part of society. So we cannot possibly look on the organism as being able to function in isolation. So this organism here labeled "Fritz Perls" is a living sum of processes, of functions, and these functions are always related to something of the world he has, the world that we try to describe with the word *now*. The *now* is the world in which we live. And this organism is distinguished from this thing called "chair" by having an energy in itself which operates itself. Unlike a motor car, which has to take in gas and air to make the energy that explodes in the engine, we have to secure our own energy from the food and air we take in. We have no name for the energy we create. Bergson called it *elan vital;* Freud called it *libido* or *death instinct* (he had two energies); and Reich called it *orgone*. I call it *excitement,* because the word *excitement* coincides with the physiological aspect, *excitation*.

Excitement is often experienced as rhythm, vibration, trembling, warmth. Again this excitement is not created for its own sake but in relation to the world. We take somebody's hand and we feel the hand is warm. This person is glowing toward the world. Here is another person's hand—he is cold. The frigid person always has cold hands. Of course, this person is implosive; the other explosive, outgoing. So some excitement is always being generated. Excitement = life = being. Now, excitement as such is not enough, because excitement has to energize the organism. Much of it will energize the motor system; some will mobilize the senses. These are the two systems with which we relate to the world: the motoric system of manipulation, acting, handling; and the sensory system, or system of orientation, how we see and feel.

Nature is not wasteful; nature does not just create emotions to be discharged as the excremental theory wants to have it. Nature creates emotions as a means of relating, for we were made to cope with the world in different intensities. We relate differently when we are angry than when we are loving. I believe that there is some intelligence or wisdom of the organism that differentiates these basic energies into the different tasks and functions. At present I call it the *hor-*

monal differentiation. Apparently excitement becomes tinged with some other substance—adrenalin for anger, or sexual hormones for libidinous emotions. Thus excitement varies according to the situation. When we are asleep, we need less excitement, and our metabolism goes down. In emergency situations, we can produce peaks of excitement. You know how much energy, how much violence a person can produce under a state of attack. We speak about the superhuman strength a person can have *if* he is involved, *if* he is investing his whole personality in his experience. Excitement, then, goes especially into the motoric outlet because the muscles link us with the environment. You find that in most emotional events, emotion is transformed into movement. We cannot have sex without sexual rhythm and movement; we can't grieve without our diaphragm shaking and tears being produced; we can't be joyous without dancing. So whatever excitement is necessary to create and to cope with the situation is forthcoming from the organism, and there is no unnecessary excitement. When you speak about actions that might not be acceptable by society, there is the impasse. What do you choose—to be hostile to that society or to be part of society, identified with it and willing to subdue yourself?

Comment: That's my hang-up.
  Perls: This is the existential problem for most of us. And the more insane the society, the more it is a problem. The American society dehumanizes people, making them into zombies without emotions, and the person without emotions will become like the machine. We don't live for the human being. I'm sure that

at least 70 percent of the American people are employed in the production and service of machines. So if you violate the law of the machines, the machines will hit back through those in the service of the machines. The impasse can only be solved by finding a way that is acceptable to you *and* society. For instance, I am doing something against the society I described. I toss a Trojan horse—the human soul—into that society, yet I'm being paid for it. I don't do it because I'm a reformer or a dogooder, but because I enjoy it; I'm alive doing it.

I hope you don't expect me to give you a prescription for living. All I can say is that the neurotic way of living is a very uneconomical way. It's such a waste of time, waste of energy, waste of your existence.

Comment: I can accept my actions and the consequences of them for me, but I don't live alone. My life is tied up with others, especially my family. I have no right to accept the consequences for them. Only they can do that.

Perls: I object to that phrase, "no right." This is not a legal issue. "No right" is the top-dog speaking. You see what I mean about the excitement. As such, the excitement involved with our way of living has nothing to do with society itself. It is how we regulate our lives. If you decide that you like the society and identify with it by being a well-adjusted citizen, that is your existential choice. On the other hand, if you choose to be outside society, you are not necessarily being destructive.

Comment: You're making my greed show, because I want it both ways.

Perls: So you want it both ways. And you reproach

me as if you are a bad man because you want it both ways. This is how you are. Eat *and* have. Everybody plays the role he plays; everybody is what he is. Nobody can at any given moment be different from what he is *at that moment*. If somebody comes to me and complains that his role is being depressed and he doesn't like it, then I can show this person that he is playing the depression game. He has a choice: he can play top-dog with another person and depress that person or depress himself. If this is the game he wishes to play, fine. If he wants to play this game the other way round by being nasty and depressing other people, fine. Or he may dislike certain people and go around depressing them, and so feel fine. In other words, all I can do is possibly to help people to reorganize themselves, to function better, to enjoy life more, to feel—and this is very important—to feel more real. What more do you want? Life is not violins and roses.

IV

I will conclude by discussing some ways you can continue your own growth, so you can help yourself to become aware. Now as long as we are aware, we are always aware *of something*. Sometimes the awareness is so dim that we are in a kind of trance, but basically we are always experiencing something. Even when the antiawareness forces are at work, as in sleep or fainting, very often some message is coming through, such as a dream. What we are aware of is always the message of the unfinished situation. Usually an unfinished situation is very pressing if you allow nature to take its course. If you have a letter to answer, then this letter is on your conscience not just on your desk. The situation demands to be finished.

We can use this demand for self-therapy in the form of meditation. There are many forms of meditation, and people do not understand how they differ. Many people think that meditation takes place in the realm of thoughts and ideas. When I talk of meditation, I do not mean this kind of game. To use the kind of meditation I mean is very difficult—it may take years to accomplish, especially if you are a talker. Usually people are either talkers or listeners; very few are both. People often say, "I told myself . . ." or "I said to myself . . . ," but they seldom say, "I listened to myself." The kind of meditation I suggest is learning to listen to your thinking. You can hear yourself thinking, and listen until you can hear whether *you* are talking or *somebody else* is talking.

You will find it very difficult to get the basic energy into your ears instead of your fantasy throat. But when you can do this, you will realize a very peculiar phenomenon—that is, in spite of being alone, all this thinking is essentially a substitute for encounters. It is an inner world or stage that replaces the external world or stage. But if you do not listen, you will not realize that you are always talking to somebody, even if it is as vague as talking to the world. You may be telling people what they should do or defending yourself, or manipulating somebody or impressing someone.

This is nothing especially new, but it is in this process that we come across the unpleasant experience, the block, the status quo that prevents us from becoming truly substantial and growing up. And this is where we can accomplish a great deal deliberately.

It's very peculiar that we can become spontaneous only by utmost discipline. It is an absolute paradox. And absolute discipline is required in getting the antidote for our phobic attitude. The antidote is to become interested in your negative emotions. If you develop a kind of scientific objectivity, or a willingness to suffer yourself and focus on whatever unpleasant situation that might come up, then you come across the blocks for further development. I would say that one of the most important kinds of unpleasantness is boredom, so much so that I think that one of the hell gates that leads to maturity, to *satori*—the great awakening—is the ability to stay with boredom, not to try to jump out of it, do something interesting, or use it for complaining.

But boredom is not the only unpleasantness we encounter. There is also the feeling of frustration. It is true that in a final sense, we cannot possibly be frustrated. Either our self-esteem or the organism will always find some way out. If a girl rejects us, we will try to get a substitute satisfaction by becoming vindictive or violent. Whatever frustration we encounter, there is always some alternate attempt to get satisfaction. The only trouble is that if the key doesn't fit the lock, the door doesn't open—the substitute does not lead to the completion of the situation. But staying with frustration, staying with boredom, will evoke organismic self-regulation. It is like a cut. *You* cannot do anything to heal the cut. The organism takes over. You might prevent further complications by sterilizing the cut, but if you leave it alone, nature will take care of it. If you want a better understanding of the simplicity of life and environment, I recommend a pocketbook entitled *The Top of the*

World,[*] which says much about the beauty and the meaningfulness of life. At one point an Eskimo says, "The white people are peculiar people. They bring their laws along but leave their wives at home."

You see, we clog up our lives with so many thousands of unnecessary unfinished situations. If you want to play the role of a lady, you must have a beautiful costume for this role. So you go out and buy it, or cut up pieces of cloth, and sew them together just so, in a fashionable way. But then, this costume is not finished in time, so you get angry, and so on. And think of all the other props—all for what is an unnecessary role!

If you can stay with your feelings of unpleasantness, you will find that situations tend more and more, quicker and quicker, to be finished or discarded as events that merely clog up your life. Therapists quickly become aware of how people clog up their lives by dragging unpleasant parents around with them. Well of course we are not Eskimos; we do not just put parents on sleds and let them freeze to death. But we can say, "I'm a big boy now. I don't need you."

Begin meditation by closing your eyes and just listening to your own thinking, whatever you are saying to yourself. Then, when you learn to listen, the next step is to produce a therapist. If you like me, take me, and have encounters with Fritz; take whomever you choose, it does not matter. By choosing your therapist and having him respond to you in what you are saying, you will be amazed at how much you know, at how much you can actually help yourself, at how much self-support you will discover. You will also be

---

[*] Hans Ruesch, *Top of the world*. New York: Pocket Books, Inc., #50198.

amazed to realize how much you have played stupid and helpless and phony rather than finding your self-support. You see, the psychoanalytic idea of transference is this: transference is the historical repetition of what has been. I look upon it as resentment of what it has not been.

Usually, the patient expects the therapist to give him what he is missing, to fill his holes. By playing therapist to himself, he is capable of filling his own holes. I am sure you know only too well the projection mechanism, what patients imagine, and project onto you. If you make them play at giving what you are supposed to give them, then they can reown what they have disowned—for instance, the power they hand over to others.

You can save yourself much strain and stress while doing therapy by withdrawing as often as possible. Most therapists think that they have to stay in contact with the patient all the time. But the two extremes of contact and withdrawal are both pathological. If you always hang on and cannot let go, you are fixated. If you are completely withdrawn and out of touch, then you are isolated. I can give you a simple example: A clenched fist is not a hand. A flat palm with rigidly outstretched fingers is not a hand. *This* is a hand—moving, changing, doing many things, and varying its position and movement. Similarly the heart is not a heart in its extension or in its contraction, but rather in its rhythm of contraction and relaxation. So contact with the world is a rhythm. At times it is a confluence, a oneness; at other times, isolation. As an example, sometimes you want to say something but a word is missing. You withdraw to your fantasy dictionary, find the right word, then you come back. Or perhaps you see someone and don't know what to say, so you withdraw and rehearse, then come back into contact.

As for the fixation, the deliberate energy that is called attention is very short-lived. The organism has inexhaustible awareness but it does not produce much deliberate energy. For example, if you try to concentrate on a red object, you immediately start to produce antiawareness in the form of a neutralizing color. When you look away or close your eyes you see green instead of red, indicating that you should have withdrawn from the red sooner and looked at something else. So, if you feel compelled to listen to all the garbage your patients say, especially if they are trying to bore you, hypnotize you, put you to sleep, you will be exhausted by the end of the session or of the day. But if you allow yourself to withdraw when there is no interest, you will find yourself immediately involved again when something of interest occurs. Again, if you trust the wisdom of the organism, you will be amazed at how much working capacity you have. Many times, when a group or an individual is bored or withdrawn, I will ask everyone to withdraw in fantasy.

Question: Is it possible to use some of the techniques you have talked about in a group situation?
Perls: Of course. In fact, I think that individual therapy is obsolete, that it should be the exception rather than the rule. There are certain situations when somebody in the group is not ready to be open with the group. In that case individual therapy is indicated. But workshops are, both financially and in regard to personal development, much more feasible.

Consider how much you learn in a group from indirect participation.

Question: Do you have any suggestions that would help a group to function? Can a group function without a leader?

Perls: I think a group can function well without a leader if the group will agree to some basic rules and everyone watches to insure that the rules are being followed. Here are some of the basic rules: (1) Be alert when you leave the *now*, and always go back to the *now* in the sense of both the open now and the hidden now of fantasies. (2) Forbid the use of the word *it*. (3) Encourage everyone to change nouns into verbs. (4) Never gossip about any person who is not present. Bring the absent one into an encounter by having the speaker play both roles. (5) Never force a confession. Never force anyone to say something that he does not want to say, or intrude into him. Merely deal with objections and have them expressed. (6) Give support by helping the person find his own support—by asking, "How do you. . .?" rather than saying, "Do this." These are some of the attitudes that will facilitate maturation.

Question: Will you say something about *why*?

Perls: The word *why* is the infantile approach of explanation. *Why* cannot lead to understanding. There may be one exception—when you use *why* to mean *for what purpose*. But when *why* is used for causality, it is covering up the issue with computing and rationalization. Explanation prevents understanding. The great danger you encounter as therapists is that you were trained to play the interpretation game, and the assumption of this game is that you know something about the other person and that it will help him if you tell him. Sometimes that is correct. Sometimes you do actually see what is going on. Then you might not do great harm, unless you are premature in telling him something that he is not ready for. But *anything* you can do to help the other person *discover himself* is always good. Only what we discover ourselves is truly learned.

Question: How can the therapist use himself in trying to help the patient come to terms with himself?

Perls: By being open and honest. Freud was not able to be open, and his problem got changed into a technique that took many years to correct. What happened was similar to a friend in South Africa who sent a very delicate cup to Japan to have a copy made, since the Japanese are very good at copying things. He ordered many dozens of these cups. When they arrived, all the cups arrived with handles—not attached. What had happened was that the handle of the original cup had broken off in the mail, and the Japanese copied the cup exactly as it was, in two pieces. This is similar to what happened in psychotherapy. Freud had a deep phobia. He was embarrassed to look into anybody's face or to be stared at, so he avoided the situation by putting the patient on a couch and sitting behind him. Soon this symptom became standard procedure, like the broken handle. Now we have to do the opposite. We have to make a big fuss and discover the obvious—a new type of therapy called "encounter therapy." We have finally remembered that it seems only natural that we have eyes to see the other person, that we can talk directly to him, etc.

In an encounter we must be aware of the polarities because everything, every energy is differentiated into opposites. We have many opposites: right and left, top-dog and under-dog, sadist and masochist. We try to integrate the opposed events and see how they fit until we find the center. We can be alert and have perspective only if we have a center. If we lose the center, we are out of balance.

Question: Will you talk about right and left as opposites?

Perls: The right hand is usually the motoric, male, aggressive side that wants to control, to determine what is, to decide what is "right." The left side is the female side; it is usually poorly coordinated. *Left* means *awkward* in many languages: *gauche* in French, *linkinch* in German. When there is a conflict between emotional life and active life, there is neurosis. When the male and female side fight with each other, this uses up energy in inner conflict and frustration and games and so on. But when both power and sensitivity are working in coordination, there is genius. Every genius in literature has this female component integrated with the male, and every female genius has a strong male component. An important aspect of training in Zen is training for alertness, which involves really having a center so that one can always be alert to what is going on. Ultimate awareness can only take place if the computer is gone, if the intuition, the awareness is so bright that one really comes to his senses. The empty mind in Eastern philosophy is worthy of highest praise. So lose your mind and come to your senses.

3
GESTALT THERAPY: A BEHAVIORISTIC PHENOMENOLOGY

Elaine Kepner and Lois Brien

It seems generally agreed now that human problem behavior is learned, and that psychotherapy is essentially a reeducational or learning process. Usually the use of such terms as *learning* and *behaviorism* implies that man is simply a collection of conditioned responses to environmental stimuli. We believe with Anderson (1968) that

> The behavior of human beings . . . is adequately accounted for only in terms of a radically different conception of the nature of man. Man is a creature, with a sense of self. Given this sense of self, he is able to carry on internal dialogues with himself, and he does so during practically every waking moment [p. 1].

In this article, we shall be translating Gestalt therapy into a behavioristic-phenomenological framework. That is, we propose to consider phenomenological events as actual behaviors.

Since our only access to experience is through some form of behavior, be it verbal or nonverbal, the Gestalt therapist considers *all* that is going on in a person—what he is thinking, feeling, doing, remembering, and sensing—as the data of behavior. This does not imply that Gestalt therapy is a form of behavioristic therapy (via the model of Wolpe, Goldiamond, etc.). We use the language of behavioristic learning theory because it allows us to refer to experiential events in operational terms and provides principles that account for changes in a subject's feelings, perceptions, and actions. Whether this translation will serve its function remains to be seen. As Scriven (1964) says, "The test as to whether a vocabulary imparts a new and genuine understanding is its capacity to predict new relationships, to retrodict old ones and to show a unity where there was a previous diversity [p. 183]."

BEHAVIORISM AND PHENOMENOLOGY: TWO APPROACHES TO LEARNING

A brief description of learning theory seems in order to set a background for this analysis. Learning theory is used here as a generic term designating a number of different systems developed by psychologists to account for the acquisition of knowledge and/or the emergence of new responses. Historically, psychology has approached this subject from two different views: the tradition of associationism, which today can be referred to as *behaviorism*, and the schools of introspection, functionalism, and Gestalt psychology, which may be grouped under the heading of *phenomenology* or *existentialism*.

Neither behaviorism nor phenomenology are in themselves psychological systems. Rather, they are approaches or methods in psychology for describing and studying the crucial variables which relate to and account for behavior. All learning theories take as their major function the specification of stimulus conditions that determine behavior. Both the behaviorist and the phenomenologist consider learning to be a lawful phenomenon whose laws can be discovered. Since learning is an internal state and not directly observable, the behaviorist studies a response or performance as an indicator of learning. The phenomenologist, on the other hand, studies learning as well as other behaviors through the individual's report of sensory, perceptual, or cognitive data.

There are a number of different theories. What they share in common is a language that emphasizes operational definitions of specifiable behaviors and a concern with the role of reinforcement or reward as a determinant of behavior. The behavioristic psychologist further believes that observable behavior is the only legitimate subject matter of psychology, and the only criterion against which the outcome of any experimental procedure, including psychotherapy, can be evaluated.

The phenomenologist, on the other hand, considers all that goes on inside a person—that is, his sensations, perceptions, cognitions—in a word, his experiencing—as valid psychological data, even though these events cannot be verified but must be inferred and labeled as hypothetical constructs by another person. Thus changes in such constructs as self-concept, or self-awareness, or ego-control are acknowledged as valid psychological data and valid criteria against which the outcome of therapy can be appraised.

Contemporary behaviorism and phenomenology are showing evidences of convergent thinking. For example, several learning theorists, notably, Miller, Tolman, and Skinner, have moved away from an almost exclusive concern with the environment (that is, with objective, observable, publicly verifiable behavior) to include internal psychological events as stimuli governing or shaping behavior. Osgood proposes a two-stage model of behavior utilizing an implicit stimulus-producing response assumed to mediate between observable S and observable R, yielding: S-r-s-R. The r-s refers to a covert process and might represent, for example, a listener's meaningful reaction to something just said (r) and the self-stimulation or thinking that the reaction triggers (s), both of which might lead to some overt responding.

This model is an attempt to overcome some of the limitations of the single-stage S-R behavioral model, chiefly its failure to handle symbolic processes such as ideation, cognition, and meaning. In this type of paradigm, phenomenological events can be regarded as intervening variables or internal mediating responses. Skinner (1964), in a discussion of public and private events in psychology, stated: "It is particularly important that a science of behavior face the problem of privacy. An adequate science of behavior must consider events taking place within the skin of the organism, not as physiological mediators of behavior, but as part of the behavior itself [p. 84]."

Concerning this same issue of private events in psychology, Homme (1965) coined the word *coverant* as a contraction of *covert-operant*. In Homme's words, "Coverants are events the laymen call mental. These include thinking, imagining, reflecting, ruminating, relaxing, day-dreaming, fantasying, etc. Difficulties in the control of one or the other of the coverant class undoubtedly underlie a good many behavioral or personality disorders [p. 502]."

To summarize, what seems to characterize the present scene is an increasingly fruitful dialogue between behaviorism and phenomenology. What seems to be developing is a view that "Man is at once both a whole being and a collection of habits and behaviors: that man's total being can be seen as a product of the interplay between molar self and the specific acts and habits that fill in the mosaic of daily living [Truax, 1967, p. 150]."

EXPERIENCE AS BEHAVIOR

Liverant (1965) has pointed out that:

> At its most primitive level, experience (as is usually understood) is involved whenever any organism reacts to any stimulus. As a consequence of learning (i.e., as a result of an organism's interactions with his environment), these experiences are undergoing continuous alteration which in some deterministic fashion affects an arbitrarily selected (by the observer) end-state called a response. Viewed in this manner, all learning formulations deal with experience [p. 4].

Verbal reports then are the direct tie to this experience.

In Gestalt therapy we treat the phenomenology of the person—that is, his sensations, perceptions, thoughts, visualizations, etc.—as behaviors. In Skinnerian terms these could be called *internal mediating responses* or in Hommeian terms, *coverants*. We could then translate self-awareness as used in Gestalt therapy as a process by which these coverants are made observable to the subject and observer; that is, the therapist. In other words, in Gestalt therapy we make observable or visible the phenomenal world of the subject. As Perls (1951) has pointed out:

> We emphasize that in all types of activity, whether it be sensing, remembering, or moving, our blind-spots and rigidities are in some aspect aware and not completely buried in an inaccessible unconscious. What is necessary is to give whatever aspect *is* aware more attention and interest so that the dim figure will sharpen and become clear against its ground. We can, at least, be aware that there *is* a blind-spot, and, by working alternately on what we can see or remember and on the muscular manipulations by which we *make* ourselves blind, we can gradually dissolve the blocks to full awareness [p. 117].

In the Gestalt approach, then, work in the present, in the here and now, is designed to produce observable behavior rather than merely to lead the person to talk about what he is thinking. The questions which guide the therapist are *not*, "Why are you behaving this way," but "What are you doing?" "How are you doing it?" "What is it doing for you to behave this way?"

Learning, Personality Theories, and Personality Change Strategies

As we have seen from the discussion of learning theory, learning is considered to be a relatively stable change in behavior, through practice, over time. Or, to put it more simply, learning is a change in behavior as a result of experience. As such, learning has a place in personality theory and in psychotherapy.

Personality theories have two major functions: meaningfully to describe a person as he is, and to explain how and why he has become this way. These explanatory concepts, as Gendlin (1964) pointed out, tell us what prevents an individual from changing or being changed by experience. In other words, people somehow learn to be the way they are, and personality theories tell us something about how they got to be that way. Psychotherapy is essentially a process designed to change the individual in a meaningful way. The strategies employed in psychotherapy to effect change are usually based on a theory of personality, but the overall aim is to enable the individual to learn new ways of thinking, feeling, and behaving. To put this into a learning framework, we could say that the psychotherapy strategies differ depending on what the particular personality theory sees as the crucial determinants of behavior.

For example, psychoanalytic personality theory explains behavior, particularly maladaptive or neurotic behavior, on the basis of past learnings. Psychoanalytic therapy then deals with the past, with the stimulus history of the client. Through the techniques of free association and dream interpretation, he learns to understand better how he came to be the way he is. The analysis of the transference relations with the therapist enables the client to discover how he still continues to behave as if the past existed. The discovery of reality comes about through new learning in his relationship with the nonpunitive person of the analyst.

The behavior therapists, on the other hand, focus on the actual behavior or symptom that is causing the chief problem for the client. If the therapy is based on operant principles, new and appropriate behavior is rewarded when it occurs. Old and inappropriate responses are extinguished either through punishment or nonreward.

The existential-therapists consider the important determinants of behavior to lie inside the person, and thus they focus on the client's phenomenology, that is, the internal events, or his inner world of experience.

GESTALT THERAPY AND PHENOMENOLOGICAL LEARNING

The aim of Gestalt therapy is to develop more "intelligent" behavior; that is, to enable the individual to act on the basis of all possible information and to apprehend not only the relevant factors in the external field, but also relevant information from within. The individual is directed to pay attention at any given moment to what he is feeling, what he wants, and what he is doing. The goal of such direction is noninterrupted awareness. The process of increasing awareness enables the individual to discover how he interrupts his own functioning. These interruptions can be thought of as the resistances, or the evidence of resistances. What is being resisted is the awareness of the needs that organize his behavior. Awareness in the present then becomes a tool for uncovering those needs and for discovering the ways in which the individual prevents himself from experiencing the needs.

Because of the centrality of the concept of "awareness," Gestalt therapists call attention to the manner in which a person blocks or interrupts his communications, either with his internal self-system or with the interpersonal system. Awareness of the block can be facilitated by directing attention to what his body is doing, what his mind is doing, and what is or is not going on between people (*motoric, symbolic, and interpersonal* behaviors).

Motoric behavior refers to the language of the body and may be seen in how the client looks, how his voice sounds, how he is sitting, what parts of his body are moving. This is direcly observable behavior, and the client's attention is directed to what he is doing. For instance, the therapist might initiate body work by saying, "Close your eyes and pay attention to your bodily sensations. Concentrate on them. What do you feel in your body? Can you stay with that?" Or the therapist might observe some movement in the client and begin there.

Focusing on a client's motoric behavior may, for example, call attention to the manner in which he is blocking his anger from awareness and from overt expression. In learning terms, the coverant, anger, is then labeled and identified as belonging to the self. Such identification makes possible a congruent and appropriate expression of the feeling.

Symbolic behavior refers to "mental events" such as thinking, imagining, daydreaming, etc. Such behavior is not directly observable by the therapist, but the client's attention may be directed toward his own phenomenology, that is, toward what he is *feeling*, chiefly by way of fantasy or actual visualization. Gestalt therapists are especially interested in the client's symbolic representations as these are the coverants that determine his overt behavior. Visualization may involve imagining a dialogue with another person or with a whole cast of characters. In working with visualization, the client is instructed to stay with the imagined situation and to let it change as it will.

A Behavioristic Phenomenology

The therapist then deals with the client's feelings, movements, etc., in relation to the visualization as it is emerging. For example, one client, in visualizing an encounter with his father-in-law, has a fantasy about being pursued by Indians. As the fantasy develops, he is able to turn around and shoot back, thereby saving himself. The visualization was a symbolic representation of a problem; it showed his initial avoidance of it by running away, and his possible solution, namely, confronting the pursuer and asserting himself. By making these coverants overt, the client was able to discover an alternative response to avoidance.

Interpersonal behavior refers to those behaviors which bridge the psychological contact boundaries between separate organisms. The person has certain functions by means of which he contacts others, for example, seeing, hearing, touching, vocalizing, etc. If we see one of the basic purposes of therapy as being a return to contact with others, then it becomes especially important that the client become aware of how he is blocking contact and that he experiment with interpersonal behaviors that increase contact.

By experimenting, a client can discover how he keeps himself apart from others. For example, a woman who believed herself to be inferior was able to test the reality of this concept with other group members. She discovered that although she may have felt inferior to others in the group in some ways, she also felt adequate in relation to them in other ways.

Experiments in the here and now permit the client to observe, cognize and specify his coverants. Much of our behavior is under the control of these coverants. What is learned by experiencing is what governs behavior. In other words, the individual learns what it is he is doing, or not doing, that prevents him from being in contact with himself and with others. Such awareness means that he can choose to continue the behavior or to change it.

Thus we may view human problem behavior, that is, "pathology," as learned behavior and psychotherapy as essentially a reeducational process. All psychological learning theories attempt to specify the variables that determine behavior. The behaviorist is primarily concerned with and attempts to account for external events, that is, for stimuli and responses. The phenomenologist, on the other hand, assumes certain "givens" about the nature of man and is concerned with what goes on inside the person, that is, with the rich, variegated, and elusive internal world of the individual. The behavioristic phenomenologist deals with this world of personal experiencing in such a way as to make it external, overt, specifiable, and communicable.

REFERENCES

Anderson, Henry. Toward a sociology of being. *Manas*, 1968, *21* (3).

Brien, Lois. The behaviorist's approach to learning. *Ohio Journal of Speech and Hearing*, 1966, 2, 74–79.

Deese, James. *The psychology of learning*. New York: McGraw-Hill, 1958.

Gendlin, Eugene T. A theory of personality change. In P. Worchel and D. Byrne (Eds.), *Personality change*. New York: John Wiley & Sons, 1964.

Hill, Winifred F. *Learning*. San Francisco: Chandler Publishers, 1963.

Homme, Lloyd E. Perspectives in psychology: XXIV,

Control of coverants, the operants of the mind. *Psychological Record*, 1965, *15*, 501–511.

Kepner, Elaine. Application of learning theory to the etiology and treatment of alcoholism. *Quarterly Journal of Studies on Alcohol*, 1964, *25*, 279–291.

Koch, Sigmund. Psychology and emerging conceptions of knowledge as unitary. In T. W. Wann, (Ed.), *Behaviorism and phenomenology*. Chicago: University of Chicago Press, 1964. Pp. 1–45.

Liverant, Shephard. *Learning theory and clinical psychology*. Washington, D.C.: Clearing house for Federal Scientific and Technical Information, Defense Documentation Center, AD 612–126, 1965.

May, Angel E., and Ellenberger, H. F. (Eds.), *Existence*. New York: Basic Books, 1958.

Mednick, Sarnoff A. *Learning*. Englewood Cliffs, N.J.: Prentice-Hall, 1964.

Michael, Jack, and Meyerson, Lee. A behavioral approach to counseling and guidance. In R. L. Mosher, et al. *Guidance: An examination*. New York: Harcourt, Brace, and World, 1965.

Osgood, C. E., and Miron, M. S. (Eds.), *Approaches to the study of aphasia*. Urbana: University of Illinois Press, 1963.

Perls, Frederick, Hefferline, R. F., and Goodman, Paul. *Gestalt therapy*, New York: Dell, 1951.

Scriven, M. Views of human nature. In T. W. Wann (Ed.), *Behaviorism and phenomenology*. Chicago: University of Chicago Press, 1964.

Skinner, B. F. Behaviorism at fifty. In T. W. Wann (Ed.), *Behaviorism and phenomenology*. Chicago: University of Chicago Press, 1964.

Spence, Kenneth W. Behavior theory and conditioning. New Haven, Conn.: Yale University Press, 1956.

Truax, Charles B., and Carkhuff, Robert R. *Toward effective counseling and psychotherapy: Training and practice*. Chicago: Aldine, 1967.

4
PRESENT-CENTEREDNESS: TECHNIQUE, PRESCRIPTION, AND IDEAL

Claudio Naranjo

Psychoanalysis borrowed a haughty axiological neutrality from that complex cultural entity of our times called science. Like science, it prided itself on being "unbiased" by values, this being an aspect of what is generally understood as its "objectivity." Yet, the valuation of aloofness or noncommitment is in itself a value orientation, after all, and in the light of this the objectivity of science entails a built-in self-deception. As Laing (1960), put it:

> It may be maintained that one cannot be scientific without retaining one's "objectivity." A genuine science of personal existence must attempt to be as unbiased as possible. Physics and the other sciences of things must accord the science of persons the right to be unbiased in a way that is true to its own field of study. If it is held that to be unbiased one should be "objective" in the sense of depersonalizing the person who is the "object" of our study, any temptation to do this under the impression that one is thereby being scientific must be rigorously resisted. Depersonalization in a theory that is intended to be a theory of persons is as false as schizoid depersonalization of others and is no less ultimately an intentional act.

Although conducted in the name of science, such reification yields false "knowledge." It is just as pathetic a fallacy as the false personalization of things [p. 24].

That psychoanalysis entails an underground of values amounting to a tacit philosophy may be revealed by any inquiry into the language, themes, and statements in a standard psychoanalytic publication, especially if this is carried out with an anthropological eye. Yet a characteristic of such an underground of beliefs is to be informal and claim nonexistence. Explicitly, psychoanalysis is a science, and its application an art; it is a theory of the mind and, particularly, a theory of the psychoneuroses.

Gestalt therapy, in contrast to psychoanalysis, has little to add to a dynamic interpretation of psychopathological phenomena. It is a "therapy" more than a theory, an art more than a psychological system. Yet, like psychoanalysis, Gestalt therapy involves a philosophical underground. More than that, it rests on an implicit philosophical posture which is transmitted from therapist to patient or trainee by means of its procedures without need of explication. In addition, I would like to suggest that the experiential assimilation of such implicit *Weltanschauung* is a hidden key to the therapeutic process. This amounts to the claim that a specific *philosophy* of life provides the background for Gestalt therapy just as a specific *psychology* provides that for psychoanalytic therapy.

The transmission of certain attitudes through the use of the tools characteristic of this approach may be likened to the process whereby a sculptor creates a form with the tools of his art. In both instances the content transcends the instruments, although the instruments have been conceived for its expression. Unfortunately, it is one of our human weaknesses to trust that formulas and techniques will do everything for us, as is shown by the history of every cult, where truth petrifies into rigid forms.

In calling the philosophy of Gestalt therapy "implicit" I am not saying that it is, as in psychoanalysis, covert. It is *simply* implicit, for the Gestalt therapist places more value in action than in words, in experience than in thoughts, in the living process of therapeutic interaction and the inner change resulting thereby than in influencing beliefs. Action engenders substance or touches substance. Ideas can easily float by, cover up, or even substitute for reality. So nothing could be more remote from the style of Gestalt therapy than preaching. Yet it involves a kind of preaching without injunctions or statements of belief, just as an artist preaches his world-view and orientation to existence through his style.

MORALITY BEYOND GOOD AND EVIL

"Good" and "evil" are suspicious to the Gestalt therapist, who is used to perceiving most of human advice as subtle manipulation, discussion on moral issues as self-justification and rationalization of needs, and statements of worth or worthlessness as overgeneralizations and as projections of personal experience onto the environment—all done to avoid responsibility for the person's feelings and reactions. As Perls (1953, 1954) put it:

> Good and bad are responses of the organism. We say, "You make me mad." "You make me feel happy." Less frequently, "You make me feel good." "You make me feel bad." Among primitive people such

phrases occur with extreme frequency. Again we use expressions like "I feel good," "I feel lousy," without considering the stimulus. But what is happening is that an ardent pupil makes his teacher feel good, an obedient child makes his parents feel good. The victorious boxer makes his fan feel good, as does the efficient lover his mistress. A book or a picture does the same when it meets your aesthetic needs. And *vice versa:* if people or objects fail to meet needs and produce satisfaction, we feel bad about them.

The next step is that instead of owning up to our experiences as ours, we project them and throw the responsibility for our own responses onto the stimulus. (This might be because we are afraid of our excitement, feel that we are failing in excitement, want to shirk responsibility, etc., etc.) We say the pupil, the child, the boxer, the lover, the book, the picture "is" good or bad. At that moment, labeling the stimulus good or bad, we cut off good and bad from our own experience. They become abstractions, and the stimulus-objects are correspondingly pigeon-holed. This does not happen without consequences. Once we isolate thinking from feeling, judgment from intuition, morality from self-awareness, deliberateness from spontaneity, the verbal from the non-verbal, we lose the Self, the essence of existence, and we become either frigid human robots or confused neurotics.

In spite of such views on good and bad, Gestalt therapy abounds in injunctions as to the desirability of certain attitudes toward life and experience. These are *moral* injunctions in the sense that they refer to the pursuit of the good life. Even though the notion of morality in common parlance has come to indicate a concern about living up to standards extrinsic to man, it is possible that all the great issues in morality once originated in a humanistic ethic where good and evil were not divorced from man's condition. Thus the concept of *righteousness* in Judaism, that eminently law-giving religion, once indicated the condition of being in tune with God's law or will, which we may understand as similar to that alluded to by the nontheistic Chinese as living in the Tao—following one's proper *Way*. So it would seem that what in a living vision of life is seen as right, just, adequate, or good, after being expressed in laws, turns against man and enslaves him by claiming some authority greater than himself.

If we want to list the implicit moral injunctions of Gestalt therapy, the list may be longer or shorter according to the level of generality or particularity of our analysis. Without claiming to be systematic or thorough, here are some that may give an impressionistic notion of the style of life entailed:

1. Live now. Be concerned with the present rather than with past or future.
2. Live here. Deal with what is present rather than with what is absent.
3. Stop imagining. Experience the real.
4. Stop unnecessary thinking. Rather, taste and see.
5. Express rather than manipulate, explain, justify, or judge.
6. Give in to unpleasantness and pain just as to pleasure. Do not restrict your awareness.
7. Accept no *should* or *ought* other than your own. Adore no graven image.
8. Take full responsibility for your actions, feelings, and thoughts.
9. Surrender to being as you are.

The paradox that such injunctions may be part of a moral philosophy that precisely recommends giving up injunctions may be resolved if we look at them as statements of truth rather than duty. Responsibility, for instance, is not a *must*, but an unavoidable fact: we *are* the responsible doers of whatever we do. Our only alternatives are to acknowledge such responsibility or deny it. All that Gestalt therapy is saying is that by accepting the truth (which amounts to a nonundoing rather than a doing) we are better off—awareness cures. Of course, it cures us of our lies.

I think that the specific injunctions of Gestalt therapy may in turn be subsumed under more general principles. I would propose the following three:

1. Valuation of actuality: temporal (present versus past or future), spatial (present versus absent), and substantial (act versus symbol).
2. Valuation of awareness and the acceptance of experience.
3. Valuation of wholeness, or responsibility.

None of the three broad life-prescriptions of Gestalt therapy listed above is the direct opposite of any world philosophy that I am aware of, although the emphasis on personal responsibility runs counter to the authoritarian streak in most mass religions. Instead, the value-orientation of Gestalt therapy is the opposite of many people's implicit philosophy of life—a philosophy that falls into familiar cultural concepts. Thus an opposite to the valuation of actuality can be found in traditionalism with its emphasis on subordinating present actions to the past, whether in the form of dead ancestors, cultural heritage, or the opinion of the aged. Also opposite to it is the future-orientation of technological societies, such as the United States. Kluckhohn (1959) has proposed time orientation as a basic issue for the understanding of values in a culture.

An opposite to the valuation of awareness and experience is the common trait that the authors of *The Authoritarian Personality* (1950) call *anti-intraception*, which they find typical of the fascist mind. This is an opposition, dislike, and rejection of the tendency to be interested in what we call "the inner life," whether in oneself or others. A typical statement endorsed by such people is, for instance, that "when a person has a problem or worry, it is best for him not to think about it, but to keep busy with more cheerful things."

The tenet of responsibility in Gestalt therapy also finds more support than challenge in the world of philosophy, but it contradicts the prevalent assumption of a divine authority *outside* the individual—in kings, priests, parents, or scientists—which is responsible for the choice of the individual's course of action or orientation. It also contradicts our common perception of ourselves as helpless playthings of accident and circumstances rather than creators of our destiny.

In the following pages I will consider in some detail one of the aspects of actuality, in itself one aspect of the philosophy of life of Gestalt therapy. In choosing *living-in-the-moment* as a theme, I am not implying that this is more important than the issues of consciousness or responsibility, but only limiting the scope of this paper to the subject on which I feel most inclined to write at the moment. I think, too, that whatever the point of departure, the content will be somewhat similar, for the three issues are only superficially distinct. On close examination we may discover, for instance, that the question of actuality is not only related to the valuation of present tense and present locus, but also to the valuing of concrete reality, sensing and feeling rather than thinking and imagining, to awareness, and to self-determination. More specifically, I hope that the following pages will show that the willingness to live in the moment is inseparable from the question of openness to experience, trust in the workings of reality, discrimination between reality and fantasy, surrender of control and acceptance of potential frustration, a hedonistic outlook, and awareness of potential death. All these issues are facets of a single experience of being-in-the-world, and looking at such an experience from the perspective of present-centeredness rather than other conceptual vantage points amounts to an arbitrary choice.

PRESENT-CENTEREDNESS AS TECHNIQUE

Although the *hic et nunc* formula recurs in scholastic literature, the relationship of the here and now to contemporary psychotherapy has been the outcome of a gradual evolution.

Psychoanalysis began with a past-oriented approach. Freud's discovery of free association had its origin in his experience with hypnosis, and his first explorations into the method were in the nature of an attempt to do away with the trance state and yet elicit the same clues for the understanding of his patient's past. He would, in those days, pose a question to the patient and ask him to report the first thought that came to his mind at the moment of touching his forehead. With increasing experience, he found that he could omit the touch on the forehead and also the question, and regard instead every utterance as an association to the preceding one in the spontaneous flow of thoughts, memories, and fantasies. At the time, this was to him no more than the raw material for an interpretive endeavor, the most precious associations being those related to the patient's childhood. His assumption then was that only by understanding the past could the patient be free from it in the present.

The first step toward an interest in the present in psychoanalysis was Freud's observation of "transference." Insofar as the patient's feelings toward the analyst were understood as the replica of his earlier feelings toward parents or siblings, the understanding of the therapeutic relationship became at once significant to the understanding of the still basic issue of the patient's past.

At the beginning, the analysis of transference was still subservient to retrospective interpretation, but we may assume that it became increasingly valued in its own right, for the next step was a gradual shift in stress from past to present, not only with respect to the material being examined but as the very goal of understanding. So although at first the analysis of the present was a tool or a means for the interpretation of the past, many today regard the analysis of childhood events as a means toward the understanding of *present* dynamics.

The lines of development have been multiple. Melanie Klein, for instance, retains an interpretational language based on assumptions about early childhood experience, but the trend of her school, in actual practice, is to focus almost exclusively on the understanding of the transference relationship. A similar focus on the present was carried by Bion into the group situation.

Wilhelm Reich's shift toward the present was the outcome of his shift of interest from words to action, the goal in his character analysis becoming that of understanding the patient's *form* of expression rather than the content of his speech. There can be no better way of doing so than by observing his conduct in the ongoing situation.

A third contribution to the valuing of the present in the therapeutic process was made by Karen Horney, touching on the very foundation of the interpretation of neuroses. In her view, emotional disturbances that originated in the past are sustained *now* by a false identity. The neurotic once sold his soul to the devil in exchange for a shining self-image, but he is still choosing to respect the pact. If a person can understand how he is burying his true self in this very moment, he can be free.

The growing emphasis on present-orientation in contemporary psychotherapy can be traced to the impact of two other sources aside from psychoanalysis: encounter groups, which are becoming increasingly widespread: and the Eastern spiritual disciplines, with Zen in particular having contributed to the shaping of Gestalt therapy into its present form.

There are at least two ways in which present-centeredness is reflected in the technical repertoire of Gestalt therapy. One is the outspoken request to the patient to attend to and express what enters his present field of awareness. This will most often be coupled with the instruction to suspend reasoning in favor of pure self-observation. The second is the *presentification* of the past or future (or fantasy in general). This may take the form of an inward attempt to identify with or relive past events or, most often, a reenacting of the scenes with gestural and postural participation as well as verbal exchanges, as in psychodrama.

Both techniques have antecedents in spiritual disciplines older than psychotherapy, and it could not be otherwise, given their importance. Presentification is found in the history of drama, magic, and ritual, and in the enacting of dreams among some primitive people. Dwelling in the present is the cornerstone of some forms of meditation. Yet both presentification and dwelling in the present find in Gestalt therapy a distinctive embodiment and form of utilization that deserve discussion at length. In the following pages I will concentrate on the approach called *the exercise of the continuum of awareness*. Since it is very much like a meditation translated into words, and its role in Gestalt therapy is comparable to that of free-association in psychoanalysis, I will deal with it mostly in comparative terms.

Gestalt Therapy and Meditation

The practice of attention to present experience has had a place in several traditions of spiritual discipline. In Buddhism it is a corollary of "right-mindfulness," one of the factors in the "Noble Eightfold Path." An aspect of right-mindfulness is the practice of "bare attention":

> Bare Attention is concerned only with the *present*. It teaches what so many have forgotten: to live with full awareness in the Here and Now. It teaches us to *face* the present without trying to escape into thoughts about the past or the future. Past and future are, for average consciousness, not objects of observation, but of reflection. And, in ordinary life, the past and the future are taken but rarely as objects

of truly *wise* reflection, but are mostly just objects of day-dreaming and vain imaginings which are the main foes of Right Mindfulness, Right Understanding and Right Action as well. Bare Attention, keeping faithfully to its post of observation, watches calmly and without attachment the unceasing march of time; it waits quietly for the things of the future to appear before its eyes, thus to turn into present objects and to vanish again into the past. How much energy has been wasted by useless thoughts of the past: by longing idly for bygone days, by vain regrets and repentance, and by the senseless and garrulous repetition, in word or thought, of all the banalities of the past! Of equal futility is much of the thought given to the future: vain hopes, fantastic plans and empty dreams, ungrounded fears and useless worries. All this is again a cause of avoidable sorrow and disappointment which can be eliminated by Bare Attention [Nyaponika Thera, 1962, p. 41].

Past and future do not qualify as "bare objects" in that they are in the nature of imagining, but are also to be avoided because dwelling in them entails a loss of freedom: illusion ensnares us in its recurrence. As Nyaponika Thera (1962) says:

Right Mindfulness recovers for man the lost pearl of his freedom, snatching it from the jaws of the dragon Time. Right Mindfulness cuts man loose from the fetters of the past which he foolishly tries even to reinforce by looking back to it too frequently, with eyes of longing, resentment or regret. Right Mindfulness stops man from chaining himself even now, through the imaginations of his fears and hopes, to anticipated events of the future. Thus Right Mindfulness restores to man a freedom that is to be found only in the present [p. 41].

The most important practice related to the view in the quotation above is that form of meditation the Chinese call *we-hsin* (or idealessness), which consists, as Watts (1950) puts it, in the ability to retain one's normal and everyday consciousness and at the same time let go of it.

> That is to say, one begins to take an objective view of the stream of thoughts, impressions, feelings and experiences which constantly flows through the mind. Instead of trying to control and interfere with it, one simply lets it flow as it pleases. But whereas consciousness normally lets itself be carried away by the flow, in this case the important thing is to *watch* the flow without being carried away . . . one simply accepts experiences as they come without interfering with them on the one hand or identifying oneself with them on the other. One does not judge them, form theories about them, try to control them, or attempt to change their nature in any way; one lets them be free to be just exactly what they are. "The perfect man," said Chuang-tzu, "employs his mind as a mirror; it grasps nothing, it refuses nothing, it receives but does not keep." This must be quite clearly distinguished from mere empty-mindedness on the one hand, and from ordinary undisciplined mind-wandering on the other [p. 176].

The practice of attention to the present in the context of Gestalt therapy is very much like verbalized meditation. Moreover it is a meditation carried into the interpersonal situation as an act of self-disclosure. This permits a monitoring of the exercise by the therapist (which may be indispensable to the inexperienced) and may also add significance to the contents of awareness.

I would not doubt that the search for words and the act of reporting can interfere with certain states of mind; yet the act of expression also adds to the exercise in awareness, beyond its being merely a means of information for the therapist's intervention. At least the following advantages of communicated awareness over silent meditation may be listed:

1. The act of expression is a challenge to the sharpness of awareness. It is not quite true to say that we know something but cannot put it into words. Of course, words are mere words and we can never *put* anything into words; yet, within limits, clarity of perception goes together with the ability to express, an artist being a master in awareness rather than a skilled patternmaker. And in art, as in psychotherapy, the task of having to communicate something involves having to really look at it rather than dreaming about looking.
2. The presence of a witness usually entails an enhancement both of attention and of the meaningfulness of that which is observed. I think too that the more aware an observer is, the more our own attention is sharpened by his mere presence, as if consciousness were contagious or one person could not as easily avoid seeing what is exposed to the gaze of another.
3. The contents of consciousness in an interpersonal setting will naturally tend to be that of the interpersonal relationship, whereas the solitary meditator focused on the here and now will systematically fail to find such contents in his field of awareness. Since it is mainly the patterns of relating and the self-image in the process of relating that are disturbed in psychopathological conditions, this factor looms large in making the here-and-now exercise a therapy when in the I-thou setting.
4. The interpersonal situation makes present-centeredness more difficult, for it elicits projection, avoidances,

and self-delusion in general. For instance, what for the solitary meditator may be a series of observations of physical states may, in the context of communication, become embedded in a feeling of anxiety about the therapist's eventual boredom, or in an assumption that such observations are trivial, or that they show the patient's essential barrenness. The elicitation of such feelings and fantasies is important.

a. If present-centeredness is a desirable way of living which is usually marred by the vicissitudes of interpersonal relationships, the challenge of contact entails the ideal *training* situation. I would like to invite the thought that the practice of living in the moment is truly an *exercise* and not merely an occasion for self-insight. Just as in behavior therapy, this is a process of desensitization in the course of which a person becomes free of the central conditioning of avoiding experience, and he learns that there is nothing to fear.

b. Related to the above is the fact that it is precisely the awareness of the difficulties in present-centeredness that can provide the first step toward overcoming them. Experiencing the compulsive quality of brooding or planning may be inseparable from an appreciation of the alternative to them, and of a true understanding of the distinction between these states of mind and present-centeredness.

5. The therapeutic context allows for a monitoring of the process of self-observation, whereby the therapist brings the patient back to the present when he has been distracted from it (that is, from himself). There are two main ways of doing this. The simplest (aside from merely reminding him of the task) is to call his attention to what he is doing unawares, by directing his attention to aspects of his behavior that seem to be automatic response patterns or to clash with his in-

tentional actions. Simply being mirror to him may serve to bring into focus his relationship to himself and his actions in general:

P.: I don't know what to say now. . . .
T.: I notice that you are looking away from me.
P.: (Giggle.)
T.: And now you cover up your face.
P.: You make me feel so awful!
T.: And now you cover up your face with both hands.
P.: Stop! This is unbearable!
T.: What do you feel now?
P.: I feel so embarrassed! Don't look at me!
T.: Please stay with that embarrassment.
P.: I have been living with it all my life! I am ashamed of everything I do! It is as if I don't even feel that I have the right to exist!

An alternative to this process of simply reflecting the patient's behavior is that of regarding the occasions of failure in present-centeredness as cues to the patient's difficulties (or rather, living samples thereof), just as in psychoanalysis the failure to free-associate is the target of interpretation. Instead of interpretation, in Gestalt therapy we have explicitation: the request that the patient himself become aware of and express the experience underlying his present-avoiding behavior. One of the assumptions in Gestalt therapy is that *present-centeredness is natural:* at depth, living in the moment is what we want most, and therefore deviations from the present are in the nature of an avoidance or a compulsive sacrifice rather than random alternatives. Even if this assumption were not true of human communication in general, it is made true in Gestalt therapy by the request that the patient stay in the present. Under such a structure, deviations may be understood as failures, as a sabotaging of the intent, or as distrust in the whole approach and/or the psychotherapist.

In practice, therefore, the therapist will not only coach the patient into persistent attention to his ongoing experience, but will especially encourage him to become aware and to express his experience at the point of failing at the task. This amounts to stopping in order to fill in the gaps of awareness:

P.: My heart is pounding. My hands are sweating. I am scared. I remember the time when I worked with you last time and . . .

T.: What do you want to tell me by going back to last week?

P.: I was afraid of exposing myself, and then I felt relieved again, but I think that I didn't come out with the real thing.

T.: Why do you want to tell me that now?

P.: I would like to face this fear and bring out whatever it is that I am avoiding.

T.: O.K. That is what you want now. Please go on with your experiences in the moment.

P.: I would like to make a parenthesis to tell you that I have felt much better this week.

T.: Could you tell me anything of your experience while making this parenthesis?

P.: I feel grateful to you, and I want you to know it.

T.: I get the message. Now please compare these two statements: "I feel grateful," and the account of your well-being this week. Can you tell me what it is you felt that makes you prefer the story to the direct statement of your feeling?

P.: If I were to say, "I feel grateful to you," I would feel that I still have to explain . . . Oh! Now I know. Speaking of my gratefulness strikes me as too direct. I feel more comfortable in letting you guess, or just making you feel good without letting you know my feeling.

In this particular instance we can see that the patient has avoided expressing and taking responsibility for his feeling of gratitude (because of his ambivalence, it later became apparent) and has acted out his feeling instead of disclosing it in an attempt to please the therapist rather than becoming aware of *his* desire for the therapist to be pleased.

When the patient deviates from the present, exploration of his motivation often fills gaps in awareness and leads to direct and effective expression.

T.: Now see what it feels like to tell me of your gratefulness as directly as possible.
P.: I want to thank you very much for what you have done for me. I feel that I would like to recompense you for your attention in some way . . . Wow! I feel so uncomfortable saying this. I feel that you may think that I am being a hypocrite and a boot-licker. I guess that *I* feel that this was a hypocritical statement. I don't feel *that* grateful. I want *you* to believe that I feel grateful.
T.: Stay with that. How do you feel when you want me to believe that?
P.: I feel small, unprotected. I am afraid that you may attack me, so I want to have you on my side.

We can look at the foregoing illustration in terms of the patient's initially not wanting to take responsibility for his alleged gratefulness. Finally, when he did take responsibility for *wanting the therapist to perceive him as grateful*, it became clear this was because of his ambivalence and his reluctance to tell an explicit lie (or, at least, a half-truth) and he could acknowledge his fear at the root of the whole event.

It is true that his first statement referred to the pounding of his heart and his fear, but now in speaking of the expectation that the doctor might attack him, he has gone more into the substance of his fear. Looking back at the excerpt, it seems reasonable to assume that he deviated from present-centeredness when he implicitly chose to manipulate rather than experience. Mere insistence on returning to the present could have possibly told more of the contents of his surface consciousness, but it would have failed to reveal the out-of-awareness operation of his avoidance.

The Continuum of Awareness and Free Association

Reporting the experience-at-the-moment not only holds a place in Gestalt therapy comparable to that of free association in psychoanalysis, but the difference between the two in practice is not as clear-cut as it would seem from their definitions.

In principle, "free association of *thought*" emphasizes what Gestalt therapy avoids the most: memories, reasoning, and explanations. In actual practice, however, the psychoanalytic patient may be primarily experience-centered in his communication, while a Gestalt-therapy patient may frequently deviate from the field of present sensing, feeling, and doing. Aside from the instructions given to the patient in Gestalt therapy to limit his communication to actuality and the field of immediate experience, there is a difference brought about by the therapist's approach to the patient's communication in both instances.

Let us take the case of a patient reminiscing about a pleasant event. An analyst might lead the patient to become engaged with the significance of the event remembered. The Gestalt therapist, on the contrary, will most probably attend to the missing report on *what is happening with the patient now, while he chooses to remember rather than dwell in the present.* Rather than focusing on the content of the memory, the therapist is concerned with the patient's present *action* of bringing the event to mind or reporting it.

The analyst, too, may choose to focus on the patient's present. In such a case he will most probably *interpret* the reminiscing as either a compensation and defense in face of the patient's feelings at the moment, or as a cue or indirect indication of his actual pleasurable feelings. The Gestalt therapist, on the other hand, will consider interpretations as messages to the patient's analytical mind, which must step out of reality in order to "think about" it. His efforts are in precisely the opposite direction—to minimize the current estrangement from experience involved in abstraction and interpretation. Therefore he will recruit the patient's efforts as a co-phenomenologist to the end of *observing,* rather than theorizing about or labeling this act of remembering. The awareness of "I am remembering something pleasant" is already a step beyond the act of remembering in itself, and may open up an avenue to the understanding of the actual motive or intent in the process. For instance, it might lead to the realization that "I want to make you feel that I have lots of good friends so you think that I am a great guy." Or, "I wish that I could feel as happy as I did in those days. Please help me." Or, "I am feeling very well-cared-for right now—just as on that occasion," and so on.

In fact, if the patient knew what he was doing in his actions of remembering, anticipating, and interpreting, there would be nothing "wrong" with them. The usual trouble is that such actions replace, cover up, and amount to an acting-out of an ongoing experience rather than its acknowledgement and acceptance. What is wrong is that they stem from the assumption that something is wrong, and the consciousness tends to be entrapped in them to the point of self-forgetfulness. Watts (1950) has commented that, after practicing for some time the exercise of living-in-the-moment, it will become apparent

> that in actual reality it is impossible to live outside this moment. Obviously our thoughts of past and future transpire in the present, and in this sense it is impossible to concentrate on anything except what is happening now. However, by *trying* to live simply in the present, by trying to cultivate the pure "momentary" awareness of the Self, we discover in experience as well as theory that the attempt is unnecessary. We learn that never for an instant has the time-thinking of the ego actually interfered with the eternal and momentary consciousness of the Self. Underlying memory, anticipation, anxiety and greed there has always been this centre of pure and unmoved awareness, which never at any time departed from present reality, and was therefore never actually bound by the chain of dreams [p. 179].

As soon as this is realized, he notes,

> it becomes possible once more to entertain memory and anticipation, and yet be free from their binding power. For as soon as one is able to look upon memory and anticipation as present, one has made them (and the ego which they constitute) objective. Formerly they were subjective, because they consisted in *identifying oneself* with past or future events, that

is, with the temporal chain constituting the ego. But when one is able, for instance, to regard anticipation as present, one is no longer identifying oneself with the future, and is therefore taking the viewpoint of the Self as distinct from the ego. To put it in another way: as soon as the ego's act of identifying itself with the future can be seen as something present, one is seeing it from a standpoint superior to the ego, from the standpoint of the Self.

It follows that when our centre of consciousness has shifted to the strictly present and momentary outlook of the Self, memory and anticipation guide peripheral and objective actions of the mind, and our being is no more dominated by and identified with the egoistic mode of thought. We have all the serenity, all the keen awareness, all the freedom from temporality, of one who lives wholly in the present, and yet without the absurd limitation of not being able to remember the past or to provide for the future [p. 179–186].

The Continuum of Awareness and Asceticism

In spite of the last statement, it may be a psychological truth that a person can hardly attain present-centeredness while remembering, before having known the taste of it in the easier situation of reminiscence-deprivation. The same may be parenthetically said on the matter of contacting one's experience while thinking. Ordinarily, thinking dispels the awareness of the self-in-the-activity-as-thinker and the feelings constituting the ground of the thinking-motivation, just as the sun during the daytime prevents our seeing the stars. The experience of thinking and not being lost in thought (that is, caught up in the exclusive awareness of the figure in the totality of figure-ground), is a condition that can be brought about most easily by contacting such experience-ground in moments of thoughtlessness. In this the Gestalt therapy techniques of suspending reminiscence, anticipation, and thinking fall in with the implicit philosophy of asceticism in general: certain deprivations are undergone in order to contact what is currently hidden by the psychological activity involved in the renounced situations. Thus deprivation of sleep, talking, social communication, comfort, food, or sex is supposed to facilitate the access to unusual states of consciousness but is not an end or ideal in itself.

The practice of attention to the stream of life relates to asceticism in that it not only entails a voluntary suspension of ego-gratification, but also presents the person with the difficulty of functioning in a way that runs counter to habit. Since the only action allowed by the exercise is that of communicating the contents of awareness, this precludes the operation of "character" (that is, the organization of coping mechanisms) and even *doing* as such. The practice of the now is one of ego-loss, as emphasized by Buddhism and discussed in the quotation from Watts.

PRESENT-CENTEREDNESS AS PRESCRIPTION

Not all that is of value as a psychological exercise need automatically be a good prescription for living. Free association may be a useful exercise, but not necessarily the best approach to conversation, just as the headstand in Hatha Yoga need not be the best posture to be in most of the time. To a greater or lesser extent, techniques have a potential for being carried into ordinary life, thus making of life the occasion for a growth endeavor. Yet it is not only the specific value of a certain approach that makes it appropriate as a prescription, but its compatibility with other desirable purposes in life; the degree of clash that it will bring about with the existing social structure and, especially, its compatibility with a conception of the good society. Thus the abreaction of hostility in a situation of no constraints can be of value in psychotherapy, but is this approach the one that would maximize sanity and well-being in a community? I think that opinions on the matter would be divided. They would be divided even on the question of truth. Whereas aggression tends to be socially reproved and the commandment states, "Thou shalt not kill," truth is commonly regarded as virtue, and lying a sin. One might therefore expect that the technique of self-disclosure, valuable in the context of psychotherapy, would be immediately applicable to life. Given the ordinary condition of humanity, though, truth has been and may continue to be not only uncomfortable or inconvenient but dangerous. The examples of Socrates, Jesus Christ, or the heretics at the time of the Inquisition, point out that an unconditional embracing of truth may mean the acceptance of martyrdom, for which I am sure the average human being is not ready. The desire to turn feelings into prescriptions in cases where society did not make such a project feasible has been one of the implicit or explicit rationales in the creation of special communities among those who share the goal of living for the inner quest. In such groups, sometimes veiled by secrecy, man has sought to live according to principles not compatible with other than a monastic, therapeutic, or otherwise special setting.

Humanistic Hedonism

Living in the moment, in contrast to other techniques, seems a perfectly appropriate prescription for life. Moreover, it appears to be more in the nature of a technicalization of a life formula than the prescribing of a technique. The idea of prescription may evoke images such as that of the bad-smelling tonic that children were frequently compelled to take "for their own good," before the time of gelatin capsules and flavor chemistry. This is part of a dualistic frame of mind in which "the good things" seem different from the "things for our good," and the goal of self-perfecting seems something other than "merely living."

This is not what the classic injunctions of present-centeredness convey. Take, for instance, King Solomon's "A man hath no better thing under the sun, than to eat, and to drink, and to be merry [Eccles. 15]." The character of this quotation, like that of most statements that stress the value of actuality, is hedonistic. And it could not be otherwise, for if the value of the present is *not* going to be for a future, it must be *intrinsic:* the present must contain its own reward.

In our times the hedonistic outlook seems to be divorced from and to run counter to religious feeling (just to "prescription orientation" in general). Insofar as "body" and "mind" are regarded as incompatible sources of value, idealism and spirituality tend to be associated with a grim asceticism, while the defense of pleasure is most often undertaken by the cynically practical, tough-minded, and hard-nosed "realists." This does not seem to have always been so, and we know that there was a time when religious feasts were real festivals. So, when we read Solomon's words in the Old Testament, we should not superimpose on them our present body-mind split, or the tough-mindedness with which those words are often repeated. Behind them was an outlook according to which living life and living it now was a holy action, a way in accordance with God's will.

Rarely do we find this balance of transcendence and immanence in Western thought, with the exception of remarkable individuals that seem to be marginal to the spirit of the times—heretics to the religious, or madmen to the common folk. William Blake, for instance, was such a man in claiming that "eternity is in love with the productions of time."

Even in psychoanalysis, which in practice has done much for mankind's *id*, the "pleasure principle" is looked upon as a childishness and a nuisance that the "mature," reality-oriented ego must hold in check.

Contrariwise, Gestalt therapy sees a much stronger link between pleasure and goodness, so that its philosophy may be called hedonistic in the same sense as the good old hedonisms before the Christian era. I would like to suggest the notion of humanistic hedonism, which does not necessarily entail a theistic outlook and yet seems to distinguish this approach from the egoistic hedonism of Hobbes, the utilitarian hedonism of J. S. Mill, and that of the ordinary pleasure seeker. (If at this point the reader wonders how Gestalt therapy can be called ascetic and hedonistic at the same time, let him remember that in Epicurus's view the most pleasurable life was one devoted to philosophical reflection while on a simple diet of bread, milk, and cheese.)

"Carpe Diem"

The hedonistic vein is inseparable from an intense appreciation of the present, not only in Gestalt therapy, but in the thinking of many (mostly poets and mystics) who have voiced a similar prescription. Perhaps the most insistent on this subject was Horace, whose *carpe diem* ("seize the day") has become a technical label to designate a motif that runs throughout the history of literature. Here it is in its original context:

Dom loquimur fuerbit invide aetas:
carpe diem, quam minimum credula postero.

In the moment of our talking, envious time has ebbed away,
Seize the present, trust tomorrow e'en as little as you may.

Horace's present-centeredness runs parallel to his awareness of the running away of "envious time": the irreparable loss of life that is the alternative to living in the moment. In the biblical injunction to eat, drink, and be merry, death is both the argument and the teacher. The same is true of many other statements, such as the saying, "Gather ye rosebuds while you may," or Ovid's passage in the *Art of Love*:

> *Corpite florem*
> *Qui nisi corptas erit turpiter ipse cadet.*
>
> Seize the flower,
> for if you pluck it not 'twill fade and fall.

Ovid, in particular, shares with Horace not only his hedonism and present-centeredness but his allusions to the cruelty of time: *"tempus edax rerum"* ("time devours things"). It would seem, therefore, that the prescription of living in the present goes hand in hand with the *awareness of death*—either the ultimate death or the chronic death of the moment as it becomes mere memory. In this sense it is a perception of the past as nothingness or unreality.

Awareness of potential death is also part of the spirit of Gestalt therapy, for such awareness is inseparable from human consciousness when freed from the avoidance of unpleasantness and from the veil of illusory satisfactions in unreality: wishful thinking and regressive reminiscence.

I would like to suggest that the triad of (1) present-centeredness, (2) the view of the present as a gift of pleasure, and (3) awareness of potential death or decay, amounts to an archetype: an experience for which the potentiality lies in human nature, so it need not be explained by tradition alone as is the custom among literary critics. Were it not for its archetypal substratum, the recurrent rewordings of the experience would impress us as mere plagiarism. Compare, for instance, King Solomon's and Ovid's injunctions with the following:

Catch then, oh *catch the transient hour*,
Improve each moment as it flies!
Life's a short summer, *man a flower;*
He dies—alas! how soon he flies!
                    Johnson

Gather therefore the rose whilest yet is prime,
For soon comes the age that will her pride deflowre:
Gather the rose of love whilst yet is time,
Whilest loving thou mayst loved be with equall crime.
                    Spenser, *The Faerie Queene*

Make use of time, let not advantage slip;
Beauty within itself should not be wasted:

> Fair flowers that are not gathered in their prime,
> Rot and consume themselves in little time.
> > Shakespeare, *Venus and Adonis*

> If you let slip time, like a neglected rose
> It withers on the stock with languished head.
> > Milton, *Comus*

As mentioned above, the focus of Gestalt therapy on the present is inseparable from its valuation of consciousness itself, expressed in its pursuit of relinquishing the avoidances with which our life is plagued. Not to avoid the present is not to avoid living in it, as we all too often do as a way of avoiding the consequence of our actions. Inasmuch as confronting the present is a commitment to living, it is freedom: the freedom to be ourselves, to choose according to our being's preference, to choose *our way*. Exposure to Gestalt therapy can demonstrate experientially that when the present is met in the spirit of nonavoidance—that is, with *presence*—it becomes what Dryden saw in it:

> This hour's the very crisis of your fate,
> Your good and ill, your infamy or fame,
> And the whole colour of your life depends
> On this important now.
> > *The Spanish Friar*

The issue is *now*, but we do not acknowledge it in our half-hearted way of living, thereby turning life into a deadly substitution of itself. We "kill" time or incur that "loss of time" at which "the wisest are most annoyed," according to Dante. Another way in which this particular aspect of living fully turns up in Gestalt therapy is in the *concept of closure*. In Gestalt psychology closure is applied to perception; in Gestalt therapy it is applied to action. We are always seeking to finish the unfinished, to complete the incomplete Gestalt, and yet always avoiding doing so. By failing to act in the present, we increase "unfinishedness" and our servitude to the load of the past. Moreover, as Horace puts it in one of his *Epistles,* "He who postpones the hour of living as he ought is like the rustic who waits for the river to pass along before he crosses; but it glides on and will glide on forever."

Perhaps we would not suspend life in the present if it were not for the dream of *future* action or satisfaction. In this connection the present-centeredness of Gestalt therapy bespeaks its realism in placing tangible existence and actual experience ahead of conceptual, symbolical, or imagined existence. Both the future and the past can only be alive in the present as thought forms—memories or fantasies—and Gestalt therapy aims at the subordination of these thought forms to *life*. Its attitude is the same as in J. Beattie: "The present amoment is our ain,/The neist we never saw." Or Longfellow:

> Trust no future, howe'er pleasant,
> Let the dead Past bury its dead!
> Act, act in the living Present!
> Heart within and God o'erhead.

Or in a Persian proverb versified by Trench: "Oh, seize the instant time; you never will/With waters once passed by impel the mill." Or in another, "He that hath time and looketh for a better time, loseth time."

All these statements are inspired by the apprehension of a contrast between the *livingness* of the present and the nonexperiential (therefore relatively unreal) nature of past and future:

> Nothing is there to come, and nothing past,
> But an eternal now does always last.
> Abraham Cawley

More often than not, our life is impoverished by the process of *substitution*, replacing substance with symbol, experience with mental construct, reality with the mere reflection of reality in the mirror of the intellect. Relinquishing past and future to come to the enduring present is one aspect of the prescription, "Lose your mind and come to your senses."

Present-Centeredness as Ideal
Der den Augenblick ergreift/Das ist der rechte Mann.

> He who seizes the moment is the right man.
> Goethe

The word *ideal* needs clarification. Ideals are frequently understood with a connotation of duty and/or intrinsic goodness that is foreign to the philosophy of Gestalt therapy. If we deprive an ideal of its quality of *should* or *ought*, it remains as either a statement of the desirable way to an end—that is, a prescription—or else a "rightness." By this I mean an *expression* of goodness rather than a means or an injunction: a sign or symptom of an optimal condition of life. This is the sense in which we may speak of ideals in Taoism, for instance, in spite of its being a philosophy of nonseeking. In spite of its noninjunctional style, the Tao Te Ching is always elaborating on the qualities of the sage: "For this reason the sage is concerned with the belly and not the eyes. . . . The sage is free from the disease because he recognizes the disease to be disease. . . . The sage knows without going about . . . accomplishes without any action," and so on. In the same sense, present-centeredness is regarded as an ideal in statements such as: "*Now* is the watchword of the wise."

Some recipes for better living are means to an end that differ from such an end in quality, but this is not true of present-centeredness. Here, as in Gestalt therapy in general, *the means to an end is a shifting to the end state right away:* the way to happiness is that of starting to be happy right away; the way to wisdom that of relinquishing foolishness at this very moment —just as the way to swim is the practice of swimming. The prescription of living in the now is the consequence of the fact that we *are* living in the now; this is something that the sane person *knows,* but the neurotic does not realize while enmeshed in a dreamlike pseudo-existence.

In Buddhism the now is not merely a spiritual exercise but the condition of the wise. In a passage of the *Pali Canon,* Buddha first utters the prescription:

> Do not hark back to things that passed,
> And for the future cherish no fond hopes:
> The past was left behind by thee,
> The future state has not yet come.

and then the ideal:

> But who with vision clear can see
> The present which is here and now
> Such wise one should aspire to win
> What never can be lost nor shaken.

Whereas the Buddhist version of the now injunction stresses the illusoriness of the alternatives, the Christian view stresses the trust and surrender entailed by present-centeredness. When Jesus says, "Take, therefore, no thought of the morrow, for the morrow shall take thought for the things of itself," giving the example of the lilies of the fields [Matt. 6], he is not only saying, "Don't act upon catastrophic expectations," but more positively, "Trust!" While the Christian version is framed in a theistic map of the universe, and trust means trust in the heavenly Father, the attitude is the same as that regarded as the ideal in Gestalt therapy, which may be rendered as trust in one's own capacities for coping with the now as it comes. The ideal of present-centeredness is one of experiencing rather than manipulating, of being open to and accepting experience rather than dwelling in, and being defensive in the face of, possibility. Such attitudes bespeak two basic assumptions in the *Weltanschauung* of Gestalt therapy: *things at this moment are the only way that they can be;* and *behold, the world is very good!*

If the present cannot be other than it is, the wise will surrender to it. Furthermore if the world is good, why not, as Seneca puts it, "glady take the gifts of the present hour and leave vexing thoughts." To say of anything that *it* is good is, of course, a statement alien to Gestalt therapy, which hold that things can only be good to *us*. Whether they are depends on us and what we do with our circumstances.

Our current perception of existence is full of pain, helplessness, and victimization. As Edmund Burke remarked over two centuries ago: "To complain of the age we live in, to murmur of the present possessors of power, to lament the past, to conceive of extravagant hopes of the future are the common disposition of the greatest part of mankind." In the view of Gestalt therapy, however, such complaints and lamentations are no more than a bad game we play with ourselves—one more aspect of rejecting the potential bliss of now. At depth, we are where we want to be, we are doing what we want to do, even when it amounts to apparent tragedy. If we can discover our freedom within our slavery, we can also discover our essential joy under the cover of victimization.

The whole process of estrangement from reality, as reality is given in the eternal now, may be conceived as one of *not trusting* the goodness of the outcome, of *imagining* a catastrophic experience or, at best, an emptiness for which we compensate by creating a paradise of ideals, future expectations, or past glories. From such "idols" we keep looking down on present reality, which never quite matches our constructs and therefore never looks perfect enough. This is how the question of present-centeredness ties in with accepting experience rather than being judgmental.

As Emerson said,

> These roses under my window make no reference to former roses or to better ones; they are for what they are; they exist with God today. There is not time to them. There is simply the rose; it is perfect in every moment of its existence . . . but man postpones and remembers. He cannot be happy and strong until he, too, lives with nature in the present, above time.

Searching for the ideal rose, we don't see that each rose is the utmost perfection of itself. For fear of not finding the rose we seek, we hang on to the concept of "rose" and never learn that "a rose is a rose is a rose." Our greed and impatience do not permit us to let go of the substitute through which we enjoy the reflection of reality in the form of promise or possibility, and by which we are at the same time cut off from present enjoyment. The intuition of Paradise Lost and the Promised Land is better than total anesthesia, but short of the realization that they are right here. Omar Khayyám knew well:

> Here with a loaf of bread beneath the bough,
> A flask of wine, a book of verse—and thou
>   Beside me singing in the wilderness—
> And wilderness is Paradise enow.
>
> "How sweet is mortal sovereignty!" think some,
> Others, "How blest the Paradise to come!"
>   Ah, take the cash in hand and waive the rest;
> Nor heed the music of a *distant* drum!
>
> Rubáiyát

References

Adorno, T. W., Frenkel-Brunswik, E., Levinson, D. J., & Sanford, N. *The authoritarian personality.* New York: Harper & Row, 1950.

Blyth, R. H. *Zen and Zen classics.* Vol. 1. Japan: Hokuseido Press, 1960.

Kluckhohn, F. R. Dominant and variant value orientations. In C. Kluckhohn & H. A. Murray (Eds.), *Personality in nature, society, and culture.* (Rev. ed.) New York: Knopf, 1959, pp. 342–357.

Laing, R. D. *The divided self.* Baltimore: Pelican Books, 1965.

Nyaponika, Thera. *The heart of Buddhist meditation.* London: Rider, 1962.

Perls, F. S. Morality, ego-boundary and aggression. *Complex,* Winter issue, 1953–54.

Watts, Alan. *The supreme identity.* New York: Pantheon, 1950.

5
SENSORY FUNCTIONING IN PSYCHOTHERAPY
Erving Polster

I would like to show how psychotherapy can help close the gap between a person's basic sensations and the higher experiences derived from these sensations. Identifying these basic sensations has become difficult for people because of the complexities of our society. A person may eat not only because he is hungry but also because certain tastes delight him, because it is mealtime, because he likes the company, or because he doesn't want to feel depressed or angry. His sensations are often only obscurely related to each other. What he does about the resulting muddle contributes to our current, frequently described crisis of identity because in order to know who we are, we must at least know what we feel. For example, knowing the difference between being hungry, angry, or sexually aroused surely is a lengthy step toward knowing what to do. In this interplay between feeling and doing lies the crux of our search for good living.

As conceptual background for identifying and activating sensation, I would like to introduce the concept of *synaptic experience*. The synaptic experience is an experience of union between awareness and expression. You may feel this union if you become aware, for example, of breathing while talking, of the flexibility of your body while dancing, or your excitement while painting. At times of union between intensified awareness and expression, profound feelings of presence, clarity of perception, vibrancy of inner experience, and wholeness of personality are common.

The term *synapse* is derived from the Greek word meaning conjunction or union. Physiologically, the synapse is the area of conjunction between nerve fibers, where they form a union with one another. The synaptic arc facilitates union between sensory and motor nerves, bridging the gap between these neutral structures by special, though not altogether understood, energy transmissions. The metaphoric use of the synapse focuses our attention on united sensori-motor function as represented by awareness and expression.

Various therapies differ as to their methods for bringing expression and awareness together, but most, if not all, do share in calling attention to the individual's inner processes, sometimes including sensation as well as expression. Some therapies do not acknowledge any concern with inner process (the operant-conditioning people are among them), yet they repeatedly inquire about how the patient experiences anxiety. Most therapists would agree that if a patient were, for example, to tell about his feelings of love when his mother sang him to sleep, his story would have a greater effect both for him and his listener if he were aware of his feeling. The patient, if given timely direction, may become aware of many sensory phenomena as he speaks. His body may be moist, warm, flexible, tingly, etc. The emergence of these sensations increases the restorative powers of the story because through the resulting unity of feelings and words it becomes a more nearly incontrovertible confirmation of a past love experience.

Exploring sensations is, of course, not new to psychology. Wilhelm Wundt foresaw sensory experience as the root support from which all higher feeling emerged, but his research and that of many others never had the humanistic flavor that attracts the psychotherapist. However, there are many recent humanistic views that do herald a new recognition of the power of sensation. Schachtel (1959) for one, has shown the commonality of the infant and the adult in their experience of primitive, primary, and raw sensation. He says, "If the adult does not make use of his capacity to distinguish . . . the pleasurable feeling of warmth . . . [from] perceiving that this is the warmth of air or the warmth of water . . . but instead gives himself over to the pure sensation itself, then he experiences a fusion of pleasure and sensory quality which probably approximates the infantile experience. . . . The emphasis is not on any object but entirely on feeling or sensation [p. 125]."

The child's sensation tone is the paradigm for the purity of sensory experience. Although sensations do become cluttered over the years, early experiences need not be merely infantile. In our quest for fulfillment, many of our energies are directed toward the recovery of early existential possibilities. The early innocence of sensation has been neutralized by social forces that dichotomize the child and the adult into altogether separate creatures. However, the adult is not merely a replacement for the child. Rather he is the result of accretions which need not make the character of childhood irrelevant. A child-like sense may orient and vitalize us even in the face of newly developing realities. As Perls, Hefferline, and Goodman (1951) have said about the recovery of past memories, "the content of the recovered scene is unimportant but the childish feeling and attitude that lived that scene are of the utmost importance. The childish feelings are important not as a past that must be undone, but as some of the most beautiful powers of adult life that must be recovered: spontaneity, imagination, directness of awareness, and manipulation [p. 297]."

Reports of LSD users also extoll the primacy of sensation. Alan Watts (1964) says that while on LSD he is aware of changes in his perception of such ordinary things as "sunlight on the floor, the grain in wood, the texture of linen, or the sound of voices across the street. My own experience," he adds, "has never been of a distortion of those perceptions as in looking at one's self in a concave mirror. It is rather that every perception becomes—to use a metaphor—more resonant. The chemical seems to provide consciousness with a sounding box . . . for all the senses, so that sight, touch, taste, smell, and imagination are intensified like the voice of someone singing in the bathtub [p. 120]." In our own way, we psychotherapists may also provide a sounding box for resonance, as I shall now describe.

We may start by dividing the whole range of human experience into *culminative experiences* and *ingredient experiences*. The culminative experience exists in a composite form. It is a total and united event of primary relevance to the individual. As I write these words, for example, the act of writing is the culmination of a lifetime of experiences leading to this moment and forming a part of the composite structure of writing. Furthermore, each movement of my finger, each breath I take, each tangential thought, each variation in attention, confidence, zest, and clarity join together to form the composite experience I-am-writing. As elements in the composite unit, however, each of these is an ingredient experience. These ingredient experiences frequently go unattended, but when one does explore their existence and discovers their relationship to the culminative event, one may develop a heightened experience. The gourmet does this as he tastes a sauce. Hopefully, he encounters the quality of that taste in totality, as an integrated experience. However, he also examines his experience more pointedly so that he may identify the ingredients that make up the sauce. He may identify certain herbs, a familiar wine, proportions of butter, etc. This awareness enriches him, leading him to a new dimension of taste experience. The analysis and resynthesis create a rhythm between destruction of the composite taste and re-creation of it. This reverberation between destruction and re-creation occurs over and over, helping to intensify the vibrant taste. So also, when we explore our inner sensations, we may identify the ingredients of the everyday experiences which form the substance of our lives. Enrichment occurs when there is maximal possibility for the emergence of underlying or component parts into the foreground of our knowledge. The adventure of unlimited accessibility of experience and the fluctuations between a synthesized experience and the elemental parts of our existence provides a dynamic and continually self-renewing excitement.

The recovery of this dynamic process frequently requires close attention, much as relearning to walk after an illness. Concentration is one technique for the recovery of sensation. It is well known that one must concentrate to do good work, but instructions to do so usually sound vague, moralistic, and general. Yet, concentration can be a specific mode of operation that involves giving close regard to the specific object of one's interest. It must be pointed and singleminded. When these conditions are satisfied and one's concentration is brought to bear on internal sensations, events may occur that are remarkably comparable to events arising out of hypnosis, drugs, sensory deprivation, heroic eruptions, and other conditions that take the individual out of his accustomed frame of reference. Although not usually as potent as these other conditions, a great advantage of concentration for heightening experience is that one may readily return to ordinary events and ordinary communications. Thus, one may move in and out of other modes of interaction such as talking, roleplaying, fantasy, dream work, etc., which makes it easier to accept the experience as relevant to everyday consciousness.

Moving now to the therapeutic situation itself, I shall describe the role of sensations with three therapeutic purposes in mind. They are: (1) the accentuation of fulfillment, (2) the facilitation of the working-through process, and (3) the recovery of old experiences.

First, with respect to fulfillment, there seem to be two kinds of people, the action-oriented and the awareness-oriented. Both can live rich lives if one orientation does not exclude the other. The action-oriented person who has no deep barrier to the awareness of experience will, through his actions, arouse his experience of self. The swimmer, for example, may discover many powerful inner sensations, as may the business executive who won leadership of a new company. The individual who is oriented toward awareness will find that so long as he does not exclude action, his awarenesses will direct him to action. The psychologist may write a book or create an organization, the restless person may move to another city, and the sexually aroused person may have intercourse. Psychological troubles result when the rhythm between awareness and expression is faulty.

To illustrate, an action-oriented person, a successful businessman, came to therapy because he was not experiencing fulfillment in life. Unusually vital and active, he needed to make every second count and became impatient with any moment of nonproductivity. He could not accept the accumulation of sensation, keeping always ahead of himself by prematurely discharging sensation either through action or through planning action. Consequently he was having great difficulty knowing "who I am." During the first ten sessions we talked a great deal and made some introductory explorations into his inner experience. These included certain awareness experiments and breathing exercises. Then, one day when I asked him to close his eyes and concentrate on his inner experience, he began to feel a quietness in himself and to experience a feeling of union with the birds singing outside the window. Many other sensations followed. He kept them to himself, as he told me later, because to describe them would have meant interrupting himself, a wise but atypical appreciation for feeling rather than productivity. At one point, seeing that his abdomen was not integrated into his breathing, I asked him to use his abdomen more fully, which he was readily able to do. When he did, he began to feel a new ease of breathing, accompanied by an easy strength as distinct from the impatient strength with which he was familiar. He could really tell the difference between the two kinds of strength. He said he felt like a car that had been perfectly tuned. He then left, saying he was recovering a missing link in his life. He felt as though he had *experienced* time rather than having *wasted* it.

We may illustrate our second therapeutic purpose, the facilitation of the working-through process, by the story of a woman who recently became an executive in a toy factory. Her secretary had been in her department for years, but was a disorganized and controlling person. My patient became aware that this secretary was the root of many of the previous departmental troubles and confronted her with certain departmental requirements. This was a great blow to the secretary, who suddenly looked "like a waif." My patient felt as though she were now sitting face-to-face with another part of herself. She and her brother had grown up in an impoverished section of New York and had indeed been waifs. However, since she had always nurtured her younger brother, she only saw him as a waif, not herself. In her life she had alternately supported waifs and played the waif herself.

In our talk, she realized she didn't want to be a waif any more and knew that in this confrontation with her secretary she had accepted the chance to get rid of the waif in herself and become a woman in her own right. As she told me about this, a new look came over her face, a mixture of absorption, alert introspection, and yielding to puzzlement. When I asked her what she felt, she said in surprise that she felt a tightness in her breathing and in her legs. She concentrated on these sensations and after a few moments of silence looked surprised again and said she felt a tightness in her vagina. I asked her to attend to this sensation, which she did. Again, after a few moments of concentration a brightness arose in her face, and she said the tightness was leaving. Then she seemed startled and suddenly had a deep sensation that she didn't describe but instead burst into paroxysms of crying, calling out the name of a man she loves and with whom she has for the first time had a relationship of mutuality and strength. When she looked up, there was great beauty and wholeness apparent in her. As we spoke further, she realized the importance of her confrontation with her secretary, whom she subsequently fired, and the rediscovery of her feelings about waifs. But she knew that her deepest breakthrough came with the discovery of the sensation in her vagina. The subsequent awakening of her palpable feelings of womanhood gave substance and therefore primal resolution to problems which might otherwise only be verbalized.

Finally, a third purpose served by the recovery of sensation is the recovery of old events. The unfinished situation moves naturally into completion when barriers are dissolved and when new inner stimulation propels one toward completing the unfinished business. Psychoanalysis, although differing from Gestalt therapy in many details of conceptualization and technique, has made the return of the old and forgotten a familiar expectation in psychotherapy. Although many words about the past have been spoken in therapy, these are frequently without the accompaniment of deep sensations. The next situation illustrates how sensations rather than mere words may lead the way to an old event.

A woman whose husband had died about ten years previously, had spoken about her relationship with him but had never gotten across a sense of the profundity of their experience together. In one session, a series of awarenesses evolved, including the experience of her tongue tingling, a burning feeling around her eyes, tenseness in her back and shoulders, and then dampness around her eyes. Following a lengthy sequence of these experiences, she caught a deep breath and realized that she felt like crying. There was a sense of tears in her eyes and a sensation in her throat that she could not describe. After a very long pause, she felt an itch, which she concentrated on at some length. It should be said that with each new sensation, the silence and inner concentration was lengthy, frequently lasting for minutes. Silence when joined with focused concentration has the effect of building up the intensity of feeling. Soon she began to feel itchy in many places. She found it difficult to stay with these sensations without scratching, but she did. She was feeling somewhat amused about the surprising spread of her itching sensation, but she also began to feel frustrated and sad again, as though she might cry. She talked about an irritating experience she had had the night before at the home of her parents where she had not been able to show her irritation. Then she felt a lump in her throat, and after a period of concentrating on the lump, a palpitation appeared in her chest. Her heart started beating rapidly and this made her quite anxious. She verbalized the *pump, pump, pump* sounds, then became aware of a sharp pain in her upper back. She paused at great length to concentrate on the pain in her back, then said under considerable stress, "Now I remember that horrible night that my first husband had a heart attack." Another lengthy pause followed where she appeared under great tension and absorption. Then she said in a hushed tone that she was aware again of the pain, the anxiety, and the whole experience of that night. At this point she gave in to deep, heartfelt crying, which lasted about a minute. When she finished she looked up and said, "I guess I still miss him." Now the vagueness was gone and I could experience the reality and wholeness of her relationship with her husband. The clear transformation from superficiality to depth was apparently brought on by the buildup in sensation through self-awareness and concentration, letting her own sensations lead the way rather than her ideas or explanations.

To summarize, the concept of synaptic experience provides a background for the relevance of sensation for good living and accentuates the importance of the rhythm between one's awareness and one's expression. Although it represents only part of the total therapeutic methodology, the individual's discovery of his sensations, where it becomes relevant, may lead him to an experience of fulfillment, may help complete the working-through process, and may stimulate the recovery of old events.

References

Perls, F., Hefferline, R., and Goodman, P. *Gestalt therapy.* New York: Dell, 1951.

Schachtel, E. *Metamorphosis.* New York: Basic Books, 1959.

Watts, A., A psychedelic experience: Fact or Fantasy. In D. Solomon (Ed.), *LSD, the consciousness expanding drug.* New York: Putnam, 1964.

6
THE PARADOXICAL THEORY OF CHANGE

Arnold R. Beisser

For nearly a half century, the major part of his professional life, Frederick Perls was in conflict with the psychiatric and psychological establishments. He worked uncompromisingly in his own direction, which often involved fights with representatives of more conventional views. In the past few years, however, Perls and his Gestalt therapy have come to find harmony with an increasingly large segment of mental health theory and professional practice. The change that has taken place is not because Perls has modified his position, although his work has undergone some transformation, but because the trends and concepts of the field have moved closer to him and his work.

Perls's own conflict with the existing order contains the seeds of his change theory. He did not explicitly delineate this change theory, but it underlies much of his work and is implied in the practice of Gestalt techniques. I will call it the *paradoxical theory of change*, for reasons that shall become obvious. Briefly stated, it is this: *that change occurs when one becomes what he is, not when he tries to become what he is not.* Change does not take place through a coercive attempt by the individual or by another person to change him, but it does take place if one takes the time and effort to be what he is—to be fully invested in his current positions. By rejecting the role of change agent, we make meaningful and orderly change possible.

The Gestalt therapist rejects the role of "changer," for his strategy is to encourage, even insist, that the patient *be* where and what he *is.* He believes change does not take place by "trying," coercion, or persuasion, or by insight, interpretation, or any other such means. Rather, change can occur when the patient abandons, at least for the moment, what he would like to become and attempts to be what he is. The premise is that one must stand in one place in order to have firm footing to move and that it is difficult or impossible to move without that footing.

The person seeking change by coming to therapy is in conflict with at least two warring intrapsychic factions. He is constantly moving between what he "should be" and what he thinks he "is," never fully identifying with either. The Gestalt therapist asks the person to invest himself fully in his roles, one at a time. Whichever role he begins with, the patient soon shifts to another. The Gestalt therapist asks simply that he be what he is at the moment.

The patient comes to the therapist because he wishes to be changed. Many therapies accept this as a legitimate objective and set out through various means to try to change him, establishing what Perls calls the "top-dog/under-dog" dichotomy. A therapist who seeks to help a patient has left the egalitarian position and become the knowing expert, with the patient playing the helpless person, yet his goal is that he and the patient should become equals. The Gestalt therapist believes that the top-dog/under-dog dichotomy already exists within the patient, with one part trying to change the other, and that the therapist must avoid becoming locked into one of these roles. He tries to avoid this trap by encouraging the patient to accept both of them, one at a time, as his own.

The analytic therapist, by contrast, uses devices such as dreams, free associations, transference, and interpretation to achieve insight that, in turn, may lead to change. The behaviorist therapist rewards or punishes behavior in order to modify it. The Gestalt therapist believes in encouraging the patient to enter and become whatever he is experiencing at the moment. He believes with Proust, "To heal a suffering one must experience it to the full."

The Gestalt therapist further believes that the natural state of man is as a single, whole being—not fragmented into two or more opposing parts. In the natural state, there is constant change based on the dynamic transaction between the self and the environment.

Kardiner has observed that in developing his structural theory of defense mechanisms, Freud changed processes into structures (for example, *denying* into *denial*). The Gestalt therapist views change as a possibility when the reverse occurs, that is, when structures are transformed into processes. When this occurs, one is open to participant interchange with his environment.

If alienated, fragmentary selves in an individual take on separate, compartmentalized roles, the Gestalt therapist encourages communication between the roles; he may actually ask them to talk to one another. If the patient objects to this or indicates a block, the therapist asks him simply to invest himself fully in the objection or the block. Experience has shown that when the patient identifies with the alienated fragments, integration does occur. Thus, by being what one is—fully—one can become something else.

The therapist, himself, is one who does not seek change, but seeks only to be who *he* is. The patient's efforts to fit the therapist into one of his own stereotypes of people, such as a helper or a top-dog, create conflict between them. The end point is reached when each can be himself while still maintaining intimate contact with the other. The therapist, too, is moved to change as he seeks to be himself with another person. This kind of mutual interaction leads to the possibility that a therapist may be most effective when he changes most, for when he is open to change, he will likely have his greatest impact on his patient.

What has happened in the past fifty years to make this change theory, implicit in Perls's work, acceptable, current, and valuable? Perls's assumptions have not changed, but society has. For the first time in the history of mankind, man finds himself in a position where, rather than needing to adapt himself to an existing order, he must be able to adapt himself to a series of changing orders. For the first time in the history of mankind, the length of the individual life span is greater than the length of time necessary for major social and cultural change to take place. Moreover, the rapidity with which this change occurs is accelerating.

Those therapies that direct themselves to the past and to individual history do so under the assumption that if an individual once resolves the issues around a traumatic personal event (usually in infancy or childhood), he will be prepared for all time to deal with the world; for the world is considered a stable order. Today, however, the problem becomes one of discerning where one stands in relationship to a shifting society. Confronted with a pluralistic, multifaceted, changing system, the individual is left to his own devices to find stability. He must do this through an approach that allows him to move dynamically and flexibly with the times while still maintaining some central gyroscope to guide him. He can no longer do this with ideologies, which become obsolete, but must do it with a change theory, whether explicit or implicit. The goal of therapy becomes not so much to develop a good, fixed character but to be able to move with the times while retaining some individual stability.

In addition to social change, which has brought contemporary needs into line with his change theory, Perls's own stubbornness and unwillingness to be what he was not allowed him to be ready for society when it was ready for him. Perls had to be what he was despite, or perhaps even because of, opposition from society. However, in his own lifetime he has become integrated with many of the professional forces in his field in the same way that the individual may become integrated with alienated parts of himself through effective therapy.

The field of concern in psychiatry has now expanded beyond the individual as it has become apparent that the most crucial issue before us is the development of a society that supports the individual in his individuality. I believe that the same change theory outlined here is also applicable to social systems, that orderly change within social systems is in the direction of integration and wholism; further, that the social-change agent has as his major function to work with and in an organization so that it can change consistently with the changing dynamic equilibrium both within and outside the organization. This requires that the system become conscious of alienated fragments within and without so it can bring them into the main functional activities by processes similar to identification in the individual. First, there is an awareness within the system that an alienated fragment exists; next that fragment is accepted as a legitimate outgrowth of a functional need that is then explicitly and deliberately mobilized and given power to operate as an explicit force. This, in turn, leads to communication with other subsystems and facilitates an integrated, harmonious development of the whole system.

With change accelerating at an exponential pace, it is crucial for the survival of mankind that an orderly method of social change be found. The change theory proposed here has its roots in psychotherapy. It was developed as a result of dyadic therapeutic relationships. But it is proposed that the same principles are relevant to social change, that the individual change process is but a microcosm of the social change process. Disparate, unintegrated, warring elements present a major threat to society, just as they do to the individual. The compartmentalization of old people, young people, rich people, poor people, black people, white people, academic people, service people, etc., each separated from the others by generational, geographical, or social gaps, is a threat to the survival of mankind. We must find ways of relating these compartmentalized fragments to one another as levels of a participating, integrated system of systems.

The paradoxical social change theory proposed here is based on the strategies developed by Perls in his Gestalt therapy. They are applicable, in the judgment of this author, to community organization, community development and other change processes consistent with the democratic political framework.

7
CRISIS PSYCHOTHERAPY: PERSON, DIALOGUE, AND THE ORGANISMIC EVENT

Vincent F. O'Connell

The journey which is the lived life is not an evenly spaced event in space and time as is the highway that is laid down by the engineer. It is more like music, a process of rhythm and change that unfolds in time and space, according to its own nature. This rhythm and change of life is not metaphysical, it is a concrete matter. It is an affair of the heart and the guts, of works done, of joys felt, of sufferings endured. It is also a matter of feeling. Feelings are always concrete and not metaphysical. They have to do with the heart, the blood, the muscles—with the blocks and expressions, the joys and agonies of living. Nowhere is this more evident than in the situation of crisis—that period of time wherein the person is being called on to make a step forward in his development.

In a crisis, the person comes on a crossroads. He encounters there both what he is and what he can be if he changes himself. A crisis occurs when a person is confronted by the community demands on him—when he must come to know himself as limited. Without this community processing, a person does not grow—he knows himself only as an isolated individual. The path to becoming a person and the crises of that journey are at once the hope of an individual's salvation and his purgatory also. He longs for growth, strains toward growth, yet he hangs back as well from the suffering that all growing entails. And this is how the crossroads come into being.

A person enters the crisis situation when his accustomed mode of living in the community has become less viable. This is when awareness dawns that all is not well with him. Should he heed that signal, and make the necessary changes in himself by adapting himself to the present demands, he will move forward in his development almost without hesitation or pause. Since there are inherent rigidities in personality, however, the organismic signal is sometimes ignored and the path of comfort and avoidance is chosen instead. But the processing demands continue steadily (or intermittently) until the conflict once again becomes acute—until the person's awareness of himself as a conflicted organism becomes the orienting factor in his living. Depending on who he is and how acute his suffering has become, he may at this moment come to psychotherapy for help.

What is a crisis? Paul Tillich calls it "the walk through Hell," which is apt, descriptive, and phenomenologically precise. It has been called also "the passage through fire," (Montaurier, 1966) and described as the struggle with the biblical angel—and it is all of these when it is the real crisis.

For it to be the real crisis and not merely a fantasy crisis (a matter of life and death and not merely a wish fulfillment), the person needs to be in the mode of conflict and suffering. That is what makes crisis, that the person already senses the "fire," but that he holds back from the journey in which he will be processed and changed.

Occasionally a person will attempt to go through the crisis "in his head" (as many think they can)—to be analyzing, that is, what happens at the same time it is happening. That is the fantasy crisis. And it does not foster growth in an essential way since the rational aspect of the personality inevitably takes over. To put it in another way: We may be able to cheat our way in the world of men, but we can never "cheat our way into heaven." (What I call "heaven" and others might prefer to call "reality," has nothing to do with pre-conceptions, projections, or rationalizations. That is what makes it heaven, that things are just the way they are, and none other!)

THE PATIENT AND THE PERSON

The person in crisis sweats and squirms and has his psychic balance shaken up in giving himself to the struggle, and the therapist must also expect to be processed in some measure as he takes "the walk through hell" with the person. He cannot expect to come close to the "fire" and not himself to be processed a little. He can be of no essential help if he plans to be a fence-sitter, since any kind of gamesmanship, any kind of therapeutic manipulation that is aimed at diminishing the therapist's participation, will result in closing off the growing edge of the person. This growing edge, and the work of moving toward it, depend on encounter—on the giving of oneself to what is there, while placing one's trust in the organism to guide and support the partners until they reach the core of the crisis. It is therefore necessary for the therapist to participate in what is taking place, to enable the person to stay with the growing edge of himself until the work is done.

The "walk through hell" is the encounter with one's conditioned state of behavior, with what I call "one's state of hypnosis." It involves, in brief, the processing, or changing, of those behavior patterns that are now blocking the person's coming forward in his development. It is a destructive process, in the sense that the attitudes and behaviors that no longer have survival value for the organism will be destructured so that the person may evolve new patterns of behavior more supportive of his present stage of development (Perls, 1951).

In the destructuring process, the crisis moves from the peripheral level to become a matter of acute and central concern for the person. Since he is at that moment, so to speak, in sight of the "fire," it is at that moment that symptoms also become acute. What are the symptoms? They can be legion: depressions, anxiety, fears, conversions, manipulations, helplessness, etc.—the gamut of human creativeness.

Although the person will select a limited palette to illustrate and express his suffering (and for this we can only be grateful!), an important consideration for the future progress of this therapy is the therapist's perception of symptoms. Does he, for example, interpret symptoms as forms of *resistance*—as something that interferes with the therapy process and thus something to be rid of as quickly as possible? In this case, symptoms can be a nuisance both to the person and to the therapist. Attention will be directed toward eliminating them—attention that should be directed elsewhere. Or, the therapist can view the symptoms as expressions of some pathological process going on within the person. In that event, the person is seen as "ill," and in need of some form of psychic treatment.

I prefer to approach symptoms as valuable pieces of behavior that can be turned to the person's support once he learns to decipher what he is saying on these levels of his being. Rather than being simply a reactive system of "neurotic" processes, he is seen as an open-ended center of consciousness who is moving forward in his development, as evidenced by these very symptoms. Because of this, there is no "treatment" necessary to work the crisis through. What happens is education, teaching, exploring, conversation—an experimental investigation into the person's present methods of journeying in the world with others. The person remains a *person* from the beginning to the end of the relationship. He does not need to become a *patient* for therapy to work. Indeed, the approach is oriented toward preventing the "patient syndrome" from occurring, whenever possible. The work is not something a therapist does to a patient so much as it is the study of ways of being together with this person so that ultimately he can be together with other persons.

In work with college students, this is relatively easily accomplished. Students, for the most part, are essentially "healthy" persons who can work out their living difficulties on their own. The therapist seldom needs to provide more than momentary support for the crisis situation to be resolved. His approach to them involves the same skills as are in the repertoire of any experienced therapist. But his perception of himself and his function vis-à-vis the person will need to change if he sees the patient-therapist dyad as the *sine qua non* of therapeutic movement and behavior change.

Crisis therapy in the college setting differs in important ways from crisis therapy in out-patient and in-patient settings. Whereas in the college situation we deal with, as I have said, persons who can for the most part work out their living difficulties on their own, in the latter settings we all too often meet alienated persons who have failed to resolve the crises of growth (largely because at certain crisis points there was no one to intervene to help them). In so many of the latter instances, we must deal with *scotomata* rather than *living difficulties;* and with varying degrees of hypnotic trance states (character disorders, neuroses, psychoses), which are substitute behaviors and attempts to make up for the desensitizations of the organism.

While all of these "substitute" methods of integration are to be found in the work with college students (and crisis therapy with a "borderline" person can be just as much an around-the-clock situation of hard work in the college situation as it is elsewhere), in most instances of crisis intervention with students, we begin with a person who has youth on his side and who brings the *living difficulty* with him into the therapy. The therapy can thus begin at the beginning, in the period when the conflict first arises and when it is more accessible to brief, intensive work. The student is more likely to resolve his conflict successfully. Because someone meets him at the crossroads and provides the support he needs at that time, he is strengthened enough in himself to go through the agony of being processed and changed.

TECHNIQUE, RELATIONSHIP, AND ENCOUNTER

The approach to crisis intervention may become clearer if we pose two questions I shall now attempt to answer:

1. How does the therapist involve himself in the crisis so it remains a living difficulty and does not become a "neurotic" problem in need of analysis?
2. How does the therapist enable the person to meet the crisis so that he takes "the walk through hell" and resolves the crisis for himself?

When we speak of the therapist's involvement with another person in therapy, we come to subtle and fugitive factors in the therapist's personality arising from his theory of man and of health and illness. His approach to involvement will express (and I realize this oversimplifies the matter) how much he needs to be needed by a patient, as compared with his willingness simply to be useful to this person for a time. True, the relationship begins with the essential inequality of the persons. It is the student, for example, who comes for therapy since it is he, and not the therapist, who has become problematical for himself. But being in need, or confused, or conflicted does not abridge his ability to do something for himself once there is someone who can help him for a time, unless his therapist enters the relationship with the attitude that being in a state of symptomatic crisis makes the student somehow less a person than himself. That approach seems short-sighted, for it fails to perceive that in this very inequality may reside the needed solvent of *this* person's situation. On occasion the turning point in a therapy is not reached until the therapist allows the other person to become problematical for the therapist himself!

The extent to which a therapist will permit that level of encounter to happen to him is a matter of individual choice. As I see it, the problematical aspect does not always have to fall full force on the therapist. For example, some persons in crisis need only to be taught some techniques of unblocking themselves to enable them to resolve the situation almost immediately on their own. These are the ones who, so to speak, bring "adequate relationships" with them into the crisis. They need little in the way of nourishment from the therapist's humanity since their own is not in question.

Another person may need the support of a therapeutic relationship for a limited time. He shows not only the blocking and conflict already mentioned, but the confusions and anxieties that follow when one's interpersonal supports become unstable. With these persons the approach is to strengthen them in relationship until they can be taught the techniques they need to move forward on their own. (Most students belong in this category.)

It is only with the person whose support has been radically unstable—the one who begins to fit the classification of *patient*—that the therapist's *full* participation in the phenomenal field of the other may be an essential requirement. With such a person, encounter may be the one bridge to the true state of his crisis and the means whereby his mode of hypnosis can be known and resolved.

Any long-term therapy will, of course, reach that level of involvement at which the therapist works from the approach of existential phenomenology.

But with college students it will be less frequent and then only for brief moments in an interview or for a few crucial interviews. Full participation and involvement remains for me, however, even in the most superficial of interviews, the possibility in the background of all that happens—the call to the "center" of the other, the call that enables him to see what he needs and does, and what he needs to do in the here and now to mobilize the health in himself.

I happen to believe that with this kind of involvement there is no need to fall back on the so-called therapist-patient game; the person senses this, gives up his "role" as patient, and comes out of hiding. Each interview can then offer possibility of touching the other, and of the therapist himself being touched and changed. And thus the person may come to an understanding of what he is. For want of a better formulation, I call this *the organismic event*.

THE ORGANISMIC EVENT

How does the therapist enable the person to meet the crisis so he takes the "walk through hell" and thus resolves the crisis for himself?

Participation in the phenomenal field of the other is one way to approach the person's verbal language and his body language. Are they the same voice? Is the message unified? Or is there a split between what the person says with his mouth and what he says with the rest of himself? This splitting, when it is present, is a factor in the total crisis situation; and if the person fails to understand what the many levels of the organism express, he may remain the proverbial house divided—he fails to make peace with himself.

What we see in divided communication is a form

of conflict. While the pattern of splitting and its body language may vary from person to person and from hour to hour, they are always aimed at diminishing the person's awareness of what happens to him. They may involve many kinds of alienating maneuvers, scotomizing techniques (which entail muscular contractions) as well as various forms of conditioned behaviors, which I have called hypnotic trance states. By *hypnotic state* I intend the same situation Perls calls *the state of dreaming*, but with the additional consideration here of the dreaming state as being a form of hypnosis that is based in, and kept going by, sets of conditioned behaviors. There can be literally hundreds of forms of hypnotic dreaming, all of which are a response to *fear*, be it fear of the past, fear of the present, or fear of the future. Fear in that sense is ontologically prior to anxiety, and is the base situation out of which the so-called neurotic anxieties flow. The conditioned aspect entails the patterns of behaviors the person has evolved and learned in situations of fear, particularly in those situations that were, for him, matters of life and death. The conditioned behaviors operate largely on the levels of unawareness (unconsciousness), and are well protected by the fear against penetration and unchange.

One of the forms of hypnosis that can come up again and again in crisis is the "hypnosis of the spoken word." This conditioned behavior is present when the person fails to realize that his verbal language may not be empirical fact, but mere verbalism—what Perls has aptly called "the sentence game." The person creates for himself a "verbal world," which is to say a world of words and sounds in which the musical note of the organism is heard faintly, or not at all.

When that is one of his hypnotic states, we need to jog his other senses, even to force him sometimes to be silent so that he can begin to hear once again the more central note of the organism.

As language can be a form of hypnosis when its limits are not appreciated, the precise use of language can be, paradoxically, one of the paths to liberation. I speak now of *naming* things and experiences by their given (existential) names. I am continually surprised how often it is that the person in therapy is unable to name his experiences precisely. A particularly poignant example of that difficulty can be the utter lack of contact with anxiety. Not only does a person on occasion not know its name, but he can be overwhelmed by its many manifestations; he seems never to have been taught its relationship to excitement. Such persons become "clutchers," always on the edge of the breakthrough but failing to make the step since they lack contact with adequate breathing. (While adequate breathing is one of the venerable techniques in the Gestalt tradition, it is for me a continual surprise how esoteric this elemental organismic event remains, even among psychotherapists.)

If the process of *naming* helps the person to understand *what* he experiences, the process of *localization* helps him to know *where* he experiences it. With localization we can become specific with the person, and he can learn to tune into his body language in order to mobilize his support functions more adequately.

Naming and localization, however, are no more than precise techniques that lead toward the terminus in the organismic event—that moment in which the person finally allows himself to be grasped by some aspect of his total being he has heretofore been avoiding. In crisis therapy with students, that moment is often close at hand. For that reason, techniques tend to fall somewhat into the background in deference to taking hold of the observed behavior and integrating it into the ongoing organismic flow.

It might be well at this point to stress again the experimental orientation in the Gestalt way and to note specifically that it is not a method of applying techniques. The emphasis is, rather, on the *discovery* of techniques that will enable *this* person to resolve his crisis and come forward in his development. That project is always a cooperative endeavor, one in which both persons do something with each other, in which they adopt and discard hunches and techniques with splendid abandon until the moment of breakthrough and integration happens.

One of the joys of working with college students is the aptitude and pleasure with which they adopt an experimental approach to the therapy and themselves —once they know for sure that the therapist is sincere in his attempt to discover together the student's world, to find out precisely how this world is being organized, and to see what needs to be done to make it more habitable. I have found students to be amazingly creative, quick to sense what is organismically valid, and just as quick to reject what is contrived, premature, or merely verbal. In my opinion, the new discoveries that await us in the field of psychotherapy, and in the larger area of holistic psychology as well, will come from the study of students and those like them, who work through their difficulties in the moment of their living encounter with crisis.

DIALOGUE

It may be evident at this point that I no longer use such words as *patient, symptom, treatment*. Instead, there is frequent use of such terms as *person, dialogue, encounter, organismic event*. These concepts point in the direction I find myself traveling, which is toward dialogue with the person on whatever level of himself he begins to unfold.

Treatment becomes dialogue when there is a response in kind and in sympathy. The reply, even when it is not yet the full response that will be eventually there, is still a reply. The dialogue begins always in the first tentative groping of the persons toward each other in their incompleteness.

I have found that dialogue is one of the more profound solvents for hypnosis since it provides the support that was lacking in the long ago. It introduces as well the sympathetic "vibration" the person will need if he is to enter once again (but now no longer alone) the conditioned aspect of his behavior pattern, and so try out new, unconditional behaviors.

He will need to enter the conditioned state in order to contact and assimilate, insofar as he can, these conditioned pieces of himself. In so doing, he will come to realize that on those levels of himself he is a *machine*, unfree and determined, much as the white rat in the maze who is so hypnotized by his training that he jumps to the right at the sound of the buzzer. This can be a shaking experience. It is a wrench to his accustomed perception of himself as a free individual who determines who he is and what he will be. Yet, just this wrench may be necessary if he is to awake to the mechanical factors in his living and himself, namely, those levels on which he is *an object*.

The extent to which a therapist will confront the particular person with his machine-like pattern, or even whether he touches on it at all, is determined, of course, by the particular situation. This is a matter of therapeutic intuition, and does not need further discussion here since it cuts across boundaries of schools of therapy. It is seldom very easy, however, for anyone to swallow and digest the fact that he is a machine, at least not in the beginning. Therapeutically, the primary considerations seem to be how necessary the conditioned behaviors are to the person, how available he is (with support) to assimilating the fact, and how essential it is for his growth that he know. Each person is a complex network of factors for which no static rule can be laid down.

Two things at least are patent: that not only are those levels of the person most resistant to change, but they are the realm also in which the therapist himself is in his most vulnerable state; liable himself to become hypnotized, or conditioned, by the person's conditioned behavior pattern. The early analysts understood this aspect very well, and they warned against the kind of emotional plague the person can emanate when his deep unconscious (unaware) impulses and wishes are coming into view in the therapy. This is the situation where the person becomes problematical for the therapist.

I would like to discuss just one example of this, namely, the temptation *to indulge the person on the level of his pathology*—to encourage him to remain stuck at the level of his particular problem, topic, or trauma, so that attention remains centered where it is no longer merited organismically. This is a mistake for it allows (reinforces) the student then to *invoke* his state of hypnosis (his depressions, miseries, imagined hurts, etc.) and thus to continue it. He focuses on superficial or peripheral symptoms in order to avoid the confrontation with his more basic conditioned state (with himself and what he is doing).

Paying attention so as to become aware of the phenomenal situation in the relationship is quite different from the kind of sticky preoccupation and perseveration found in the indulging mode. It is, to put it in another way, the difference between entering the person's world and wallowing with him in it. In the former instance, the lawfulness and resiliency of the organic rhythm is the orienting note: we flow with what comes and goes, as it comes and goes. In the indulging mode, there is encouraging of the continued existence of a piece of conditioned behavior the organism no longer needs. It is another instance then of a substitute act, and an instance therefore of shared hypnosis—that is, when the therapist does not mobilize himself enough to interrupt it!

I have learned, to some extent, to be sensitive to the signals of the coming hypnotic trance in myself and to pay close attention to my own support so I do not fall into dread and hatred that is often found at the core of these emotional "plague spots." I have also learned that, for me at least, the fitting response is honest and loving anger (when it comes), since in that anger there is intimate involvement and a call to the person. There is then the possibility of an encounter with what is occurring and "living it out" in the here and now.

With college students, this is often enough to bring

the *person* out of hiding. At that moment, somewhat shamefacedly, he *looks* at the person who refuses to "indulge him on the level of his pathology." It can be the beginning of the realization that there is a possibility open to him other than the one he has been following. The fact is, he may not have been able to imagine an alternative mode of behaving, and the possibility that there are other ways of relating himself to the world dawns on him with wonder and awe.

The person's motivation in indulging the "pathological" side of himself is his fear of tackling and facing his incompleteness. It is his unwillingness also to reenter those situations of indignity, confusion, and loneliness in which he feared his world would collapse—and he with it. He has an investment therefore in speaking *of* it, but not *to* it, and he thus presents his neurosis for treatment instead of himself. When someone else refuses to accept this statement of his case, when he can be persuaded to abandon for a time this mode of camouflage, there is the chance that contact and change can occur through dialogue.

But this requires a partner he can trust. He knows enough to stay away from such a processing when there is no one there with sympathy for him and understanding of his limitations and his capabilities. The work of crisis intervention entails the building of just that situation—namely, partnership.

Crisis Resolution

In choosing to emphasize the more strictly therapeutic factors in crisis intervention, I have ignored the management of the student's college environment. This is important since in many crisis situations with students, environmental pressure can be the key factor in the crisis, and its modification *is* therapeutic. The *community psychological approach* to crisis bases its approach on understanding the larger gestalt of *this* student in *this* community at *this* period of his development. And "being there for the student" is not just the matter of holding his hand for a couple of interviews in an office during the week; it is the matter also of intervening for him wherever necessary in his community, of helping to modify the responses of that community and its pressures. Being useful to him in the crisis thus means working with him on his attitudes, *and* manipulating those environmental factors which he cannot now manage successfully. We speak to him, and we speak to the significant others who are in relationship with him and with us.

The partnership with the person in crisis is, therefore, a partnership of the person and of all those who are involved in the crisis—be they professors, counselors, parents, therapists, etc. What makes the community approach work is continued conversation among the many "helping" persons who impinge on the student at this time. These persons need to talk to each other and to cooperate with each other in the primary intention of being useful to the person in crisis. Without this mutuality, crisis intervention would be a much more harrowing experience—and a saddening experience as well, since it then could evolve into chronic, long-term psychotherapy, with the therapist sitting helplessly by for a couple of hours a week, knowing all the while that there is little possibility of changing those "pathologic" factors in the student's environment which keep him coming to therapy and which he discusses each hour in helpless resignation.

When the therapist can help to modify the external pressures so they become less insistent, the person is then thrown back on himself, and his energies can be focused on the "internal" environment, on the structures within himself that need to be manipulated and changed. In that regard, I have found that full resolution of the crisis hinges generally on four existential situations: namely, (1) allowing oneself to be processed, (2) saying good-by, (3) forgiveness, and (4) allowing oneself to love.

Allowing oneself to be processed has been discussed at some length above, and it will be sufficient now simply to repeat that it entails the willingness to undergo the suffering of having one's conditioned behavior pattern made conscious and then changed. As far as I can tell, it is one of the core situations in the crisis. And it is necessary in the "evaluation period" to come to know as soon as possible what conditioned patterns keep the person stuck where he is. It is a mistake to assume the person understands these factors in his personality, even when he assures us he does—as he probably will once we begin to make the first tentative forays in their direction. He has, as I have said, an investment in keeping those unaware aspects of his personality "out of reach," even when the "health" in him struggles to contact and assimilate them.

The many Gestalt methods of resistance analysis and integration are of inestimable help at this point since they provide the needed precision in moving directly to the areas in which the conditioned behaviors are now being mobilized. With students, whose conflicts are often quite alive, these methods on occasion seem to be more magic than techniques. The ease with which a student can relieve himself of a psychic cramp only hastens his appreciation of the therapy. Since he is more liable to trust himself to an expert than to a fumbler, he moves forward more quickly from evaluation to actual work on himself when given precise orientation. I am inclined lately not to differentiate between *evaluating* the crisis and *working on* the crisis since the person's readiness to do something with his situation is mostly what counts. He can be ready in the first five minutes!

While techniques help to open up the areas for work, and integrative methods help to integrate the split-off behaviors in the person's conflicts, the *healing* he will need for full resolution of the crisis has to do with the three final situations I will now discuss.

Saying good-by is one of Perls's contributions. It rests in his more basic formulation of neurosis as an *unfinished situation*, namely, the failure to respond to a situation in terms of the "reality needs" of the time and the failure thus to assimilate and digest what was there. In failing to say good-by (to finish the situation), the person creates for himself a coterie of ghosts and phantoms which then remain on the fantasy levels of his living as various forms of plaguing, nagging, fear induction, etc.—and which show themselves in concomitant body language!

Forgiveness is a further example of finishing the situation, but with additional emphasis on giving up the resentments, hatreds, and other feelings which are the core of the conflict and which keep the person attached to his conditioned pattern. Many of the resistances a person erects against the processing of his conditioned state can rely on resentment for their motive power. Often, even when he sees how a piece of behavior is operating to his detriment and that he no longer needs it, he remains stuck in the behavior because he refuses to forgive whomever may have been the "culprit" in the long ago. Through clenched teeth, the sentence comes, "I'll never forgive you!"

I have found that abrasive irony and exaggeration to the point of absurdity is sometimes necessary to help "the blood to flow" once again. For the person often has become "bloodless" and cold (we call it hostility) as he has nursed, and cultivated, and invoked over the years the memory of the original indignity. It matters little that he sees, on one level of himself, the absurdity of keeping the situation unfinished. The fact is his heart has become cold, and his resentment closes the bridge to dialogue and reconciliation.

He will need to confront these facts if he is to change essentially. And he will very likely find out in the process that any of his present attempts to "overwhelm," or "fight," or "subdue" the resentment and hatred leads only to the conditioned behaviors becoming more nimble and powerful. He needs to be taught (and for this insight I am grateful to Herman Rednick) not to resist but gently to let go of his resenting. Another way of describing it is "to starve the conditioned behavior to drop out by nonreinforcement."

As the person learns how to let go of the resentment and to forgive, he discovers that his capacity for loving comes forward at the same time. With this he has, at last, what he needs to effectively decondition his state of hypnosis. The road ahead is then within sight and contact; it takes only a step and the crisis is finished.

Allowing oneself to love is the essential solvent of the state of hypnosis. It is the step into genuine freedom and the new beginning, since it is on the basis of loving that the mechanical factors in the personality become transparent and are eventually transcended. It is the step therefore into the liberty of the dialogue of limits, the life of community, the lived life.

The development of the loving possibilities in the person is a matter of practice and training. It is behavior that can be taught and developed, just as one can be taught to play a musical instrument, or to drive a car, or to speak Greek. But being taught how to do something involves *conversation,* in the sense that we converse with the skill we want to develop. And learning to love, to send out love to another, is also this, but something more also, since the conversation in loving is the conversation of the heart.

When we speak from the heart, we do not speak in usual terms because the speaking is then transformed, and it becomes not the *speaking out* of the everyday but the *sounding out* from the deep in oneself to the deep in the other. I have seen this in work with students. I will ask in the confused moment when the path has become obscured, "And what does your heart say to this?" And the reply sounds out, sometimes without pause or hesitation. (For when the head is doubtful, the heart often knows the way!)

It is not until the conversation reaches the heart of the crisis at hand that the speaking out becomes the sounding out to each other. When this is a shared experience from both sides, it is the genuine dialogue that Martin Buber knew—the dialogue in sympathy wherein resolution and reconciliation becomes possible.

The therapist enables the coming of dialogue in every moment of the work on the crisis when he is mindful of the difference between speaking out to the person and sounding out to him. He enables dialogue by centering himself in his heart, by mobilizing his capacity to love, no matter how diminished that capacity may be in the here and now. He works with himself and the other toward the coming of dialogue, whether the matter at hand be a technique, or a moment of waiting, or the moment of silence. Even when the appropriate response is speaking out, he holds as background for himself the possibility that in the next moment he will be changed, that he will transcend his own conditioned state and sound out to the other. This is the work of the crisis, the work of the therapy: to transform ourselves with the other, and in this sounding out to meet him and know him.

Some may view this approach as mystical. I suppose it is, insofar as we ground ourselves in the mystery we live out, a mystery we can never quite reduce to concepts and words. For each of us is spirit also while incarnated in a body, and is incomplete in himself (Marcel, 1966). We need dialogue, therefore, with the other to complement and complete ourselves in our process of creative adaptation in community. The empirical fact is this: when we send out love, when we sound out to someone with whom there is conflict, bitterness, resentment, and unfinished situations—when we sound out to that person his heart is enabled to respond.

I would not be offended if someone called this the "theological" model of psychotherapy. It is, insofar as it is a groping toward the "kingdom" that is at the center of each person and an attempt to formulate in this groping how that kingdom becomes incarnated in the shared world of the organismic event. The theological model is the model of the person's ultimate possibilities: the realm in which instinct is transformed on the basis of love, the realm in which the organism integrates itself in the world, not on the basis of substitute acts, nor with partial solutions, but in loving compassion as a free-flowing gestalt open to the world and the Self.

REFERENCES

Marcel, G. *Homo viator*. New York: Harper, 1965.

Montaurier, J. *Passage through fire*. New York: Holt, Rinehart and Winston, 1966.

Perls, F. S., Hefferline, R. F., & Goodman, P. *Gestalt therapy*. New York: Julian Press, 1951. (Republished: New York: Dell, 1965.)

CONTRIBUTORS

ARNOLD RAY BEISSER received his M.D. degree from Stanford University School of Medicine in 1949, and his Diplomate in Psychiatry from the American Board of Psychiatry and Neurology in 1958. He is currently director of the Center for Training in Community Psychiatry for the State of California Department of Mental Hygiene, and serves as associate clinical professor in the School of Medicine, Department of Psychiatry, U.C.L.A. Dr. Beisser received training in Gestalt therapy in workshops with Frederick S. Perls and James S. Simkin. He is the author of *The Madness in Sports* (Appleton-Century-Crofts), as well as numerous other articles in psychiatry and psychotherapy.

LOIS BRIEN is assistant professor of speech and communication in the Program in Speech Pathology and Audiology at Case Western Reserve University, and is a research associate at the Cleveland Hearing and Speech Center. She received her Ph.D. degree from the State University of Iowa and was a postdoctoral fellow at Western Reserve University. Dr. Brien is a consultant programmer for an N.I.H. Division of Dental Health grant, School of Dentistry, Case Western Reserve University. She is also associated with the Gestalt Institute of Cleveland.

JOEN FAGAN received her Ph.D. degree in psychology from the Pennsylvania State University. She is professor of psychology and director of clinical training at Georgia State College in Atlanta and is engaged in part-time private practice of psychotherapy. Dr. Fagan is a Diplomate of the American Board of Examiners in Professional Psychology, a member of the American Academy of Psychotherapists, and a member of the board of directors of Adanta. She has worked extensively in Gestalt therapy training workshops with Frederick S. Perls, James Simkin and others. Dr. Fagan's research interests are in innovations in psychotherapy, communication and interaction in families and awareness training.

ELAINE KEPNER received her Ph.D. in psychology from Case Western Reserve University. She is currently an assistant professor in the Department of Psychology and project director of the Community Mental Health Training Program, Cleveland College, Case Western Reserve University. She is a member of the executive board of the Cleveland Institute for Gestalt Therapy and a psychotherapist in private practice.

CLAUDIO BENJAMIN NARANJO received his M.D. from the University of Chile in 1958. He completed his residency in psychiatry at the Psychiatric Clinic, University of Chile, in 1961 and received training in psychoanalysis at the Chilean Institute of Psychoanalysis. From 1962 to 1967 he was a research psychiatrist at the Medical School of the University of Chile. During that period, Dr. Naranjo was Fulbright Visiting Scholar for the Department of Social Relations, Harvard University, and a Guggenheim Fellow for study in the psychology of values. He is currently a research associate at the Institute of Personality Assessment and Research, University of California, Berkeley, and on the staff of the San Francisco Gestalt Therapy Institute. Dr. Naranjo has led Gestalt workshops at Esalen Institute in Big Sur, California, and in San Francisco.

VINCENT FRANCIS O'CONNELL received his Ph.D. in psychology from Adelphi University in 1955 and his Diploma in clinical psychology from the American Board of Examiners in Professional Psychology in 1963. Dr. O'Connell was trained in Gestalt therapy by Frederick S. Perls in Columbus, Ohio, and at the New York Institute for Gestalt Therapy. He has held the positions of chief psychologist, Columbus Psychiatric Clinic, Columbus, Ohio; coordinator of psychological training, the Psychiatric Institute, Ohio State University; and senior staff psychologist, the Guidance Center, Inc., Daytona Beach, Florida. His current position is university psychologist of the Student Health Services, University of Florida. Dr. O'Connell is editor of the American Academy of Psychotherapists' *Newsletter*.

FREDERICK S. PERLS received his M.D. from Frederich Wilhelm University in Berlin, in 1921. He was trained in psychoanalysis at the Psychoanalytic institutes of Berlin, Frankfurt, and Vienna. He served as assistant to Kurt Goldstein in his work with brain-injured soldiers. He credited his contacts with Wertheimer, Tillich, Buber, Goldstein, and other theorists in the professional and academic circles of Germany of the twenties and thirties for inspiring the early development of Gestalt therapy. Forced to flee

Germany with his wife, Laura, he worked in private practice in Amsterdam in 1933-1934, until encroaching Nazism made it necessary to emigrate to South Africa, where he became a training psychoanalyst, served as a psychiatrist for the British Army, and established the South Africa Institute for Psychoanalysis in 1935. In 1942, he published *Ego, Hunger and Aggression* in Durban, South Africa, the first statement of the applications of the principles of Gestalt psychology to personality development and psychotherapeutic practice. In 1946, Dr. Perls and his family moved to the United States where he worked in private practice in New York, Miami, Los Angeles, Cleveland, San Francisco, and was psychiatrist in residence at Esalen Institute, Big Sur, California, where he conducted training workshops and seminars in Gestalt therapy from 1964 to 1969. He resided in Vancouver, B.C. until his death on March 14, 1970. Dr. Perls founded or helped establish the Institute for Gestalt Therapy in New York, and similar institutes in Cleveland and San Francisco. His recent work involved the extensive use of video recording of Gestalt sessions for the development of a large library of training films and transcripts. He conducted workshops in cities throughout the United States and Canada, and gave lectures and demonstrations at national professional meetings. He was coauthor, with Hefferline and Goodman, of *Gestalt Therapy* (1951), author of *Gestalt Therapy Verbatim* (1969), *In and Out of the Garbage Pail* (1969) and *Ego, Hunger and Aggression* (1969).

IRMA LEE SHEPHERD received her Ph.D. in psychology from Pennsylvania State University and is a

Diplomate in clinical psychology. She is currently professor of psychology and director of postgraduate training at the Institute for Psychological Services, Inc., Georgia State College in Atlanta, Georgia. In addition, she is engaged in part-time private practice of psychotherapy. She is a member of the executive council of the American Academy of Psychotherapists and of the board of directors of Adanta. Dr. Shepherd has been cotherapist in Gestalt training workshops with Frederick S. Perls and James S. Simkin.

RICHARD W. WALLEN died in 1968. Before his death, he was vice-president of the Personnel Research and Development Corporation of Cleveland, Ohio, and a member of the board of directors of the Cleveland Gestalt Institute.

Kirtley Library
Columbia College
8th and Rogers
Columbia, MO. 65201

DUE